It's Good to Be a Man

IT'S

A HANDBOOK FOR GODLY MASCULINITY

GOOD

MICHAEL FOSTER

TO BE

& DOMINIC BNONN TENNANT

A MAN

canonpress
Moscow, Idaho

Published by Canon Press
P. O. Box 8729, Moscow, Idaho 83843
800-488-2034 | www.canonpress.com

Michael Foster and Dominic Bnonn Tennant, *It's Good to Be a Man: A Handbook for Godly Masculinity*, ©2021, 2022 by Michael Foster and Dominic Bnonn Tennant.

This is the first paperback edition (2022): ISBN 9781954887398
Library of Congress Cataloging-in-Publication Data for the first hardback edition (2021) is available at canonpress.com.

Cover design by James Engerbretson. Interior design by Valerie Anne Bost. Printed in the United States of America.

Unless otherwise noted, all Scripture quotations are from the New American Standard Bible 1995, Copyright © 1960, 1971, 1977, 1995 by The Lockman Foundation. Used by permission.
   Scripture quotations marked NASB 2020 are from the New American Standard Bible 2020, Copyright © 1960, 1971, 1977, 1995, 2020 by The Lockman Foundation. Used by permission.
   Scripture quotations marked ESV are from the Holy Bible, English Standard Version. Copyright © 2001 by Crossway, a publishing ministry of Good News Publishers. Used by permission.
   Scripture quotations marked NIV are taken from the Holy Bible, New International Version®, NIV®. Copyright © 1973, 1978, 1984, 2011 by Biblica, Inc.™ Used by permission.
   Scripture quoations marked KJV are from the King James Version.

22 23 24 25 26 27 28   10 9 8 7 6 5 4 3 2

This work is dedicated to all the men who poured into us so we could pour into others, particularly our sons: Hudson, Athanasius, Caedmon, Miles, Morris, Cyprian, and Lochlan. May they continue to a thousand generations.

Contents

Introduction ix

1 The War between Patriarchies 1

2 Masculinity Is Very Good 17

3 Sex Is Very Good. 29

4 The War on Sex 39

5 Spiritual War & Spiritual Worship 55

6 Toxic Sexuality. 69

7 The Church Effeminate 85

8 No Father, No Manhood. 107

9 No Gravitas, No Manhood 127

10 Gravitas through Duty 143

11 How to Bear the Weight 159

12 Manhood through Mission 175

13 The Necessity of Fraternity 189

14 The Excellence of Marriage 207

Afterword. 225

Introduction

ENTERING THE WORLD OF MEN IS SUPPOSED TO be a process that slowly unfolds with the help of others. Through the oversight of a father, and the encouragement of male peers, a boy—over years—builds the confidence and mastery of manhood. But that has all been burned down. Households are broken. Fathers are absent—often not by their own choice. Male spaces for mutual encouragement are disallowed or opened to girls. Burgeoning manly desires are subdued or redirected by Adderall, video games, and pornography. Feminism reigns in the Church and the broader culture. Little boys grow up thinking there is something wrong with being masculine. Christian men are told the same thing.

Inevitably, many of us, even in adulthood, are lagging far behind where we naturally ought to be. The process of attaining manhood has been sabotaged.

This book is our contribution to the work of repair. In writing it, we did not want to create a timeless work but a timely one: our goal is to help modern Christian men understand what God made them for, and how to start doing it intentionally. We want to help *you* play your part in rebuilding what has been razed.

This is not a book about getting a girl. It is not a book about being a husband. It is not a book about being a father. It is a book about being a man. All of those other things are important to manhood, but if you don't understand what men are made for, and how God intends you to become great at being a man, none of them will matter.

God made men for dominion. That means he made you for dominion. We want you to understand what that means, and how to start taking your place, in faith, serving and fighting for God's kingdom. The world wants you distracted by grand ideas for top-down change. But God accomplishes His will mostly through works that have small, pitiful-seeming, ineffectual-looking beginnings. Consider how laughable Peter, James, and John— uneducated peasants—must have looked to the assembled cultural powers of first-century Israel and Rome. Then consider Gamaliel's wise insight about them:

> Men of Israel, take care what you propose to do with these men. For some time ago Theudas rose up, claiming to be somebody, and a group of about four hundred men joined up with him. But he was killed, and all who followed him were dispersed and came to nothing. After this man, Judas of Galilee rose up in the days of the census and drew away some people after him; he too perished, and all those who followed him were scattered. So in the present case, I say to you, stay away from these men and let them alone, for if this plan or action is of men, it will be overthrown; but if it is of God, you will not be able to overthrow them; or else you may even be found fighting against God. (Acts 5:35–39)

The walls and gates of society are built by the men who fight with God. Let us get started with that work.

1 The War between Patriarchies

PATRIARCHY IS INEVITABLE. GOD HAS BUILT IT into the fabric of the cosmos. It is part of the divine created order. You could as soon smash it as you could smash gravity. It is natural and irrevocable. Cicero was right: "Custom will never conquer nature; for it is always invincible."[1]

Men were made to rule. They always have and always will. Nothing can change that. Nothing will. It is not a question of *whether* men will be ruling, but *which* ones and *how*.

This is what patriarchy is: the natural rulership of men. The term comes from Greek and means simply "father rule."

1. Marcus Tullius Cicero, *Tusculanae Disputationes*, 5.78.

History begins with a man, Adam, commissioned to be fruitful and to multiply and to rule over the earth in God's stead. That man failed to uphold the name of his Father. *How* he ruled quickly turned bad. But *that* he ruled could not be changed. By nature, fathers rule, and he was the father of the human race. This had dire consequences for all those under his fatherhood. The Westminster Shorter Catechism explains, "The covenant being made with Adam, not only for himself, but for his posterity; all mankind, descending from him by ordinary generation, sinned in him, and fell with him, in his first transgression."[2]

Though the woman ate the forbidden fruit before the man, we did not fall in Mother Eve. We fell in Father Adam.

The failure of the first patriarch plunged mankind into sin and misery.

But God, being rich in mercy, made a promise of redemption—a promise handed down through the fathers of His people just as the curse was. He Himself told Moses, "I am the God of your father, the God of Abraham, the God of Isaac, and the God of Jacob" (Exod. 3:6). Consequently, Scripture traces the "promises given to the fathers" until their fulfillment in the finished work of Jesus

2. Question 16.

Christ (Rom. 15:8). It is through the work of the Son of Man that man is reconciled to the Father, and we can all become sons of God, fitted to rule on His behalf as Adam should have, and as Jesus now does. Fitted to be patriarchs.

Redemptive history is therefore a patriarchal history. This is why the societal structures in Scripture, too, are patriarchal: because they all are derived from the original, prototypical household. Before there were nations, there was the original ruling family—headed by Adam. Nations are headed by men because they are made up of households that are headed by men. In the same way, before there were churches, there was the original worshipping family—headed by Adam. Churches are headed by men because they are made up of households that are headed by men. Indeed, a man may not rule in the Church unless he can manage his own household well—for how else can he be competent for the greater task of managing the household of faith (1 Tim. 3:4)?

All leadership, whether in the Old or the New Testament, whether civil or domestic or ecclesiastical, is exclusively male. Mary Daly, a feminist scholar, once quipped, "The bible is hopelessly patriarchal." She was right. But it is not just the Bible. The world itself, being created by the same author, is also "hopelessly patriarchal."

In no society, anywhere or at any time, have these realities been absent . . . In every society that has ever existed one finds patriarchy (males fill the overwhelming percentage of upper hierarchical positions and all other hierarchies), male attainment (males attain the high-status roles, whatever these may be in any given society), and male dominance (both males and females feel that dominance in male-female encounters and relationships resides in the male, and society and authority systems reflect this).[3]

So, patriarchy is the natural and inevitable state of the world. But just because something is *natural* doesn't mean that it will always be *virtuous*. Good things can be perverted by sin. Whereas *unnatural* things are always evil—because they are contrary to God's design—natural things, though created good, can nonetheless be turned to unnatural ends. Homosexual desires are always wrong; heterosexual desires were designed to be good, yet every man knows how his flesh turns those desires toward that which is against God's law. For a man to be attracted to a woman is natural; for a man to lust after her is sin.

Natural things must therefore be ordered toward the ends God intended for them. They must be conformed to His law.

3. Steven Goldberg, *Why Men Rule: A Theory of Male Dominance* (Chicago: Open Court, 1933), 59, 63.

So it is with patriarchy. Male rule is natural, and so it is inevitable—but when it is not governed by God's law, it will be wicked. Because it is natural, it cannot be destroyed—but it can be twisted.

This gives birth to an evil patriarchy: the rulership of wicked fathers, who do not represent the fatherhood of God. Although our culture treats all patriarchy as evil, God's father-rule is *good*. Evil patriarchy is that which does not reflect God's loving authority. Evil patriarchy hates those under it; it is not so much anti-women as it is anti-everything, and especially anti any threat to its own power.

In fact, you can understand redemptive history through the lens of these warring patriarchies: the power of good patriarchs conflicting with the power of evil ones.

For example, it was inevitable that Egypt would be ruled by a patriarch. But it was not inevitable that Pharaoh would be good. The king who ruled in the days of Joseph gave honor to Israel and his sons. But the king who arose in the days of Moses did no such thing. He saw the sons of Israel as a threat to his reign—and he determined to do something about it. At first he tried hard labor, but when this didn't crush their spirits and prevent them from being fruitful and multiplying, he commanded the Hebrew midwives, "When you are helping the Hebrew women to give birth and see them upon the birthstool, if it is a son, then you shall put him to death; but if it is a daughter, then she shall live" (Exod. 1:16).

Pharaoh knew that the young men of Israel, unlike the women, were a threat to his reign. Why? Because all men are potential patriarchs. Men are designed for conquest and rule—and their combined strength could be sufficient to break the chain of even a mighty dynasty like Egypt. So Pharaoh tried to use the Hebrew women against the Hebrew men. But in one of the great ironic reversals of redemptive history, Shiphrah and Puah, the godly midwives, did not comply with the schemes of a corrupt ruler as Eve had done. Rather than being deceived into unwittingly abetting him, they resisted Pharaoh by deceiving *him:*

> But the midwives feared God, and did not do as the king of Egypt had commanded them, but let the boys live. So the king of Egypt called for the midwives and said to them, "Why have you done this thing, and let the boys live?" The midwives said to Pharaoh, "Because the Hebrew women are not as the Egyptian women; for they are vigorous and give birth before the midwife can get to them." So God was good to the midwives, and the people multiplied, and became very mighty. Because the midwives feared God, He established households for them. (Exod. 1:17–21)

Thus, Pharaoh was forced to find another way to murder the future patriarchs of Israel, and he "commanded all his people, saying, 'Every son who is born you are to cast into the Nile, and every daughter you are to keep alive'" (v. 22).

Young men are always the target of an evil patriarchy. Because God has made them to rule, they are a threat to existing rule. Therefore, evil patriarchs always try to do one of three things:

1. **Harness them.** Why waste all that masculine energy, after all, if it can be turned toward the ends of the evil patriarch? This is the first impulse of any patriarch, since he is a leader of men, regardless of how wicked or righteous he is. Most nations have done this to some degree, through inculturation and education—especially patriotism, military service, and formal schooling. We see Nebuchadnezzar doing this with the Israelite noblemen (Dan. 1). Our own recent history is replete with examples, from legitimate patriotism that honors the fifth commandment, to vile programs that pervert it, like Hitler Youth, or the Islamic radicalization of disaffected men in America. Pharaoh, too, tried to harness the sons of Israel; we can detect the strong cultural influence of the Egyptians in the idolatry of the Exodus generation.

2. **Pacify them.** If the energy of men cannot be harnessed by an evil patriarch, it often can be sapped by channeling it into pursuits that leave them impotent to rebel. This can be

done by putting them to work as slaves, as Pharaoh did, but often it is by offering them bread and circuses—fruitless pursuits to escape into, rather than doing the hard work of fighting. Sex is an obvious choice here, as in the case of the Philistines trying to pacify Samson through Delilah (Judg. 16:5). In our day, the technique has been perfected with porn and, to a lesser extent, video games. Men who are hooked up like junkies to the dopamine drip of virtual fornication and fake dominion are worthless for the task of being fruitful in real life and imposing genuine order on their worlds. Marx, following his father the original liar, famously said that religion is the opiate of the masses. Not so. This entire book is rooted in the reality that religion, true religion, is the one thing that sets the masses free from the actual opiates of fake dominion and fake fruitfulness. When this happens, there is only one option left for evil patriarchs:

3. **Destroy them.** Young men who cannot be harnessed or pacified must be crushed. They are too dangerous to an evil patriarchy to be allowed to live. This is why the most godless regimes are always the most murderous. Communism is well-known for its ruthless hunt for dissidents in its own ranks—typically men. Pharaoh was determined to kill every baby boy among the Hebrews—even though

it would decimate his labor force. Herod, too, sought to have the young Jesus killed by slaughtering the innocent (Matt. 2).

Throughout all of history, we see manifestations of this war between the patriarchies. Men will always rule—but which men? In an evil patriarchy, many men fail to overcome the harnessing, pacifying, and destructive forces arrayed against them. Many men fail to become patriarchs—and many more fail to become *good* patriarchs, ruling well over the domains God has given them. For many men, their authority is either taken away by those with power over them or it is twisted. Either way, whoever controls the men controls the culture.

Sometimes the way this war is waged is overt, as in the case of Pharaoh, but sometimes it is more subtle. Covert war is best exemplified by Absalom, son of David, who had his eye on his father's throne. Absalom knew the importance of men in achieving his goal. So he hatched a plot.

Men would visit Jerusalem every day to bring legal cases requiring the king's judgment. Some didn't feel heard. Maybe they were—maybe they weren't. Either way, Absalom saw an opportunity:

Absalom used to rise early and stand beside the way to the gate; and when any man had a suit to come to the king for judgment, Absalom would call to him and say, "From what city are you?" And

he would say, "Your servant is from one of the
tribes of Israel." Then Absalom would say to him,
"See, your claims are good and right, but no man
listens to you on the part of the king." Moreover,
Absalom would say, "Oh that one would appoint
me judge in the land, then every man who has
any suit or cause could come to me and I would
give him justice." And when a man came near to
prostrate himself before him, he would put out his
hand and take hold of him and kiss him. In this
manner Absalom dealt with all Israel who came to
the king for judgment; so Absalom stole away the
hearts of the men of Israel. (2 Sam. 15:2–6)

Absalom was able to steal the kingdom from
David by stealing the hearts of the men. He invested time in them, took an interest in them, sided
with them, and defended them.

Every age has its Pharaohs and its Absaloms. But
Absaloms are especially prevalent in times of dis-
ruption and disorder. They wait for a power vacu-
um created by weak and ineffectual patriarchs.

Such is our time. The Absaloms are many. And
while that is cause for concern, God is pleased to
also raise up bold and godly patriarchs. Here is one
last patriarch to keep in mind: Nehemiah.

Centuries after Absalom, that great city where he
sat in the gates was reduced to smoldering rubble.
Its walls were broken down by Nebuchadnezzar,
and its gates were burned with fire. When Nehemiah

saw it, he wept. He wept because he knew that a city is protected by its walls, and guided by the men who sit in its gates. Jerusalem had neither. She had been reduced to a chaotic ash heap: "Then I said to them, 'You see the bad situation we are in, that Jerusalem is desolate and its gates burned by fire. Come, let us rebuild the wall of Jerusalem so that we will no longer be a reproach'" (Neh. 2:17).

We find ourselves in a similar situation. Western society is burning. The structures that led to her prosperity have been broken down. You see this in many realms, but none so clearly as the state of our men. Like the inhabitants of Jerusalem in the days of Nehemiah, our men are in "great distress and reproach" (1:3).

We are living in a world of fatherless males who don't know how to rebuild the walls of society. They have become clueless bastards. They know how to build, explore, and conquer—in video games. They must turn to YouTube to learn how to jump-start a car, tie a half-Windsor knot, and do a push-up. Social skills are even harder for them. They scour the internet to learn how to stand up for themselves, make friends, and talk to women. The knowledge that is normally transmitted from father to son has been lost. They have to rediscover it for themselves.

As if being functional bastards weren't bad enough, they are being born into a radically unstable cultural situation. Technological and environmental shifts have resulted in men having such low testosterone levels that their grip strength is weaker than that of women from a generation ago. The ubiquity of porn has led to erectile dysfunction in men not even out of their twenties. Social media and dating apps have made the "relational marketplace" so extraordinarily competitive that some men just give up and either abandon the idea of sex or turn to virtual reality and even robots. Masculinity is shamed. Strong men are vilified as toxic. Those who speak out have their houses destroyed. Fathers are portrayed in mass media as unnecessary buffoons—little better than one of the kids. Anyone esteeming motherhood as foundational to femininity is canceled. Domestic violence is regarded as an exclusively male sin. No-fault divorce, welfare, and wickedly prejudicial custody laws incentivize women to leave their husbands and take everything they have—and so they do, initiating nearly 80 percent of all divorces. Male suicide rates are heading for the skies. No one cares.

All of this would have seemed absurd just fifty years ago.

Yet here we are. Our culture has become like Jerusalem, burning—and so have our men. More correctly, our *men* have become like Jerusalem, burning—and so has our culture. The men of the West have become ruined cities, and our real cities, states, and nations have followed. "Like a city that is broken into and without walls is a man who has no control over his spirit" (Prov. 25:28).

This is not primarily our fault. It is the fault of our fathers, and their fathers, and their fathers too. It is the fault of the evil patriarchs who have harnessed, pacified, and destroyed them. But it is ours to fix. We are the ones now living in burning Jerusalem, and we are the ones who must rebuild the walls. We are the ones who must overcome the evil patriarchs of our day, whether in the deep state or the media-industrial complex. We are the ones who must refuse to be turned aside to their will by deception and gaslighting, refuse to be numbed by their offers of cheap pleasure, and refuse to be cowed by their intimidation and oppression.

Jerusalem is indeed burning. Many men in the Church know it, and they are tired of living in the ash heap. The conditioning of our culture cannot conquer their masculine nature—they want to fight. But they crave guidance.

When the Babylonians burned Jerusalem, God raised up Nehemiah to rebuild it. But where are the Nehemiahs of our day? Where are the pastors who build with a trowel in one hand and fight with a sword in the other? Where are the Christian leaders who can rally men with words like this—and mean it? "When I saw their fear, I rose and spoke to the nobles, the officials and the rest of the people: 'Do not be afraid of them; remember the Lord who is great and awesome, and fight for your brothers, your sons, your daughters, your wives and your houses'" (Neh. 4:14).

The Church is not known for such men. And so in the absence of godly Nehemiahs, young men are turning to Absaloms. *Someone* must help them repair what is broken and rebuild what has been lost. The clueless bastards are groping for fathers. And so they find Jordan Peterson, Rollo Tomassi, Joe Rogan, pickup artists, and secular men's rights advocates. They discover that these men listen. These men understand. These men advocate for them and defend them. These men are trying to fight and build. They have a hammer in one hand and a firearm in the other.

And so these men steal their hearts.

The Church is in danger of losing another generation of men. We are in danger of prolonging our time in exile. We need Nehemiahs who will lead men in the work of rebuilding—but they are few. Many leaders in the Church won't even acknowledge that Jerusalem is burning at all. And the ones that do can't honestly explain why. They are blind guides, prescribing solutions that not only fail to address the core problem but create *more* of that problem.

This has created a void.

Our book is a modest contribution to filling this void with something other than unbiblical judgments from secular Absaloms. We want to rebuild the walls and reset the gates of society. This must start from within. It must start in our own lives, and then move out to reform our households, and then the household of faith. We will therefore focus on

the goodness of God's creation order, how it got all
messed up, and how you, as an individual man, can
work toward restoration. We want to restore masculine piety: the duties we have to God and neighbor
as men. Because as a man goes, so goes his household; as a household goes, so goes the Church; and
as the Church goes, so goes society.

2 Masculinity Is Very Good

GENESIS CONTAINS THE BLUEPRINT FOR RECOV-
ering manhood.

It contains the key to explaining our present cultural moment. It contains the information you need to understand women. It contains the clues necessary to interpret God's direction for your life. It contains the landmarks you need to find your way to mature manhood.

Everything is in Genesis.

To explain this, we must first ask a question.

Why did God make man?

We have found that most Christians today have no answer to this question. They may well have asked why God made *them,* but they have seldom considered this question in light of God's purpose for mankind as a whole. If pushed, they may gesture vaguely toward love as God's motive. If they are better taught, they will say for His own glory. But if you press them further, they will either run out of steam or run into error.

Part of the reason for this is that most Christians today spend very little time in Genesis. When they are not actively embarrassed by it, they are indifferent to it. Their time is spent in the New Testament. After all, isn't that God's final revelation?

Yes—but Genesis is the seed of all Scripture. Everything grows from there, including the New Testament. Without understanding Genesis, you cannot adequately understand the rest of God's word. Nor are you well-equipped to understand His creation. Genesis is the kernel from which everything grows—which is to say that *everything is in Genesis.*

Just as the seeds of Genesis take time to reach fruition in history, so they take time to reach fruition in your heart. Once you have received the implanted word (Jas. 1:21), you must tend and cultivate it before it will grow; before you can discern its full form or taste its fruit.

So why did God make man?

Then God said, "Let Us make man in Our image, according to Our likeness; and let them rule over the fish of the sea and over the birds of the sky and over the cattle and over all the earth, and over every creeping thing that creeps on the earth." God created man in His own image, in the image of God He created him; male and female He created them. God blessed them; and God said to them, "Be fruitful and multiply, and fill the earth, and subdue it; and rule over the fish of the sea and over the birds of the sky and over every living thing that moves on the earth." (Gen. 1:26–28)

You are probably so familiar with this that you didn't even bother to read it.

But do you *know* it?

Here is one way to find out: try summarizing it. What would that look like?

Maybe something like this: *God said, "Let us make man as our stand-in, to rule, rule, rule, rule, rule over everything." So God made man as His stand-in, male and female, and He told them, "Flourish and rule, rule, rule over everything."*

Notice how rulership, fruitfulness, and the image of God are thoroughly and repetitively linked. This near-laborious repetition is not because Moses needed to fill in space. It is to alert us that what is being said is really important, and to make us consider the significance of it.

The reason that God creates man on the earth, according to Genesis, is for *productive, representative rulership*. This is what it means to exercise dominion: to fruitfully order the world in God's stead.

To fallen ears this will sound impossible, but God made man to establish His own presence and rule in the physical realm. To bring heaven to earth through His living image. Look:

Having gone through the process of creating and ordering the God-sized structures of the world over the first six days, Yahweh stops and rests on the seventh. He does not order it down to the nth degree. He does not manicure every tree and shrub. He does not dam any rivers. He builds no houses. He leaves the world untamed and unrestrained, and creates just a single garden sanctuary. Then He fashions one last kind of creature—a creature suitable to continue His work, suitable to function as His creative viceroy, suitable to expand His rule across the globe. As God worked in the first week, so Adam will take over from Him in the second.

The NET Bible's translators note: "God's purpose in giving humankind his image is that they might rule the created order on behalf of the heavenly king and his royal court. So the divine image, however it is defined, gives humankind the capacity and/or authority to rule over creation."[1]

Notice also the language God uses in connection with this task: *fill* the earth and *subdue* it. We see in Genesis, in the days prior, that the world has been filled already with other life—but here we are alerted that it is not yet subdued, and that

1. Genesis 1, note 50, NET Bible, accessed August 26, 2021, https://netbible.org/bible/Genesis+1.

to subdue it, mankind will have to continue this process of filling, started by God. They will have to fill it with themselves, so that God's ordering presence can be extended into every forest, desert, plain, and tundra.

Evangelical Christianity speaks of this commission in terms of "stewardship." This is basically true, but the term stewardship mutes the far more forceful terms that God actually uses. ***"Rule* the earth,"** or "have dominion," means to reign with kingly power. It refers not just to authority, but authority backed up by might. For example:

- "One from Jacob shall have **dominion**, and will destroy the remnant from the city" (Num. 24:19; emphasis added here and below).
- "May he also **rule** from sea to sea . . . Let the nomads of the desert bow before him, and his enemies lick the dust" (Ps. 72:8–9).

"*Subdue* it" means to vanquish or even to forcefully put down. Elsewhere in Scripture it is used in reference to conquering and even enslavement:

- "Now you are proposing to **subjugate** for yourselves the people of Judah and Jerusalem for male and female slaves . . . " (2 Chron. 28:10; cf. Neh. 5:5).
- "If you will do this, if you will arm yourselves before the LORD for the war, and all of you

armed men cross over the Jordan before the LORD until He has driven His enemies out from before Him, and the land is **subdued** before the LORD, then afterward you shall return and be free of obligation toward the LORD and toward Israel" (Num. 32:20–22; cf. Josh. 18:1).

We should not conclude from this that God created us to have a *combative* relationship with the world. There is no hostility between Adam and creation; he was not to violently oppress it. This much is obvious from the fact that *all* the creation is declared very good (Gen. 1:31), and Adam was created to carry on God's very good work. God's rule is always wise, loving, and righteous. But Genesis clearly does imply that the world was needful of taming, subjugating, conquering: "The general meaning of the verb appears to be 'to bring under one's control for one's advantage.' In Gen 1:28 one might paraphrase it as follows: 'harness its potential and use its resources for your benefit.'"[2]

Again, this is dominion: fruitfully ordering the world in God's stead. While the garden in Eden was a sanctuary, Genesis does not suggest that the rest of creation was similar. The garden was bounded; the rest of the world was not gentle or soft, but wild and dangerous. Adam was made to bring it into

2. Genesis 1, note 58, NET Bible, accessed August 26, 2021, https://netbible.org/bible/Genesis+1,

submission, to order and shape it. Perhaps the garden was a kind of model for Adam of how things should look once he was finished with this commission.

It is important that Adam's task here is dominion, not just stewardship, because it calibrates our understanding of two critical things: Adam's nature, and God's. What Adam was created to do is what *we* are created to do; and the God who created him is the God who calls *us*. If Adam was made in God's image, and that image is worked out in terms of dominion—as it unquestionably is in Genesis 1— then how God exercises dominion should tell us a lot about how He expects us to image Him. We have seen that this involves bringing order by forming and filling in Genesis. But we also learn a great deal about God's dominion *throughout* Scripture. This is a point lost in modern Christianity, where the focus is almost exclusively on the model of Jesus in the gospels. But while that model is of course perfect, it is not *complete*. It is a model of God, as the second Adam, humbling Himself to correct the mistakes of the first. It is not yet a model of Him ruling over the world as Adam should have. Jesus did not take up the rule of Adam until after His resurrection from the dead and ascension into heaven (Eph.1:20–22). To see how God exercises dominion, therefore, we need to look to the rest of Scripture.

While there are many examples of dominion, the archetype which Scripture itself emphasizes is that of an ideal "apex ruler"—a sort of aspirational model for what man, at his greatest, could be. This is the model that God gives Israel as He rescues them from bondage in Egypt, to inaugurate them as a nation to bear His name. It is the model of the warrior king. *Yahweh is a man of war; Yahweh is his name,* as Moses chants in Exodus 15:3. This model is taken up again in Revelation, describing the living Christ who reigns over the world from heaven:

> And I saw heaven opened, and behold, a white horse, and He who sat on it is called Faithful and True, and in righteousness He judges and wages war. His eyes are a flame of fire, and on His head are many diadems; and He has a name written on Him which no one knows except Himself. He is clothed with a robe dipped in blood, and His name is called The Word of God. And the armies which are in heaven, clothed in fine linen, white and clean, were following Him on white horses. From His mouth comes a sharp sword, so that with it He may strike down the nations, and He will rule them with a rod of iron; and He treads the wine press of the fierce wrath of God, the Almighty. And on His robe and on His thigh He has a name written, "KING OF KINGS, AND LORD OF LORDS." (Rev. 19:11–16)

What man can read this and not feel a thrill of awe—or perhaps, for the unbelieving, a chill of fear? Yet many men today shrink from taking up the sword of the Spirit to imitate Christ and exercise dominion over the portion of the world He has delegated to their authority. Men today, trained by our culture, reserve sharp cuts exclusively for those who call us to imitate the *whole* Christ—warrior king as much as foot-washing servant. They are no longer capable of distinguishing between kings and tyrants, or warriors and bandits. Contrary to such men, Scripture shows us that God glories in exercising His might and subduing His enemies by force, and any man who removes this from his view of dominion is double-minded.

Men today desperately need to hear this message:

There is no hint in the Bible that your aggressive instincts are a result of the fall.

You are not, in other words, a defective woman. Your desire to conquer and to subdue, to hew down and to build up, to form and to shape, has nothing to do with the *curse*. It is man's natural, pre-fall, created purpose. You yearn to bend the world to your will because Adam was created to bend the world to his will. Where things go wrong is not with our natural yearnings, but with our wills themselves. Adam was made to exercise his will *on behalf of God*. This is what a son does, as we will see later on—and as we will also see, the image of God is directly connected to sonship. But Adam refused, and so we refuse. We are true sons of Father Adam, doing what he did and following in his ways. This is why we can no longer bring heaven to earth, and God had to send his own Son as a new Adam to take over that process.

Nonetheless, our masculine nature is how we are designed to image God as men. This nature must be *redeemed*, not *rejected*. Sin does not eliminate our natural inclinations; it corrupts them. In the same way, grace does not replace our natural inclinations; it restores them. When Scripture describes redeemed men as new creations (2 Cor. 5:17; cf. Rev. 21:5), it does not mean we have been changed into something entirely different, but rather into something *re*newed. As Pastor Bill Smith puts it, "The new creation is about restoring the old and taking it to its fullest glory, not growing out of it."[3]

Thus there is nothing shameful about your masculine nature: about desiring to strive, to overcome, to harness. On the contrary, masculine nature is glorious because it images the God of glory. It is what we are created to be and to do. Even now, as you seek to honor God, you are a replica made to resemble Him. How much more when you see Him face to face.

So far we have seen that God made men to rule fruitfully in God's stead, bringing His presence to

3. "Patriarchy & the Masculinity of the Passion: A Response to Peter Leithart," Kuyperian Commentary, October 13, 2020, http://kuyperian.com/patriarchy-the-masculinity-of-the-passion-a-response-to-peter-leithart.

earth as His living image. But ruling is more than the work of subduing. It also includes the work of *filling,* as God explicitly tells Adam. It includes this work not merely because Adam needs manpower for subduing, but because Adam is continuing the work of God Himself. Man cannot bring something from nothing, as God does, but he can take the raw materials that God has made and create from them something new.

A fine example of this is the one God gave Adam: a garden. Exercising dominion in a garden involves more than merely cutting back existing plants, pulling out the ones you don't want, and dividing the ones you do into neat areas. It also includes "seed work": husbanding the plants to be more productive or tasty or beautiful, cultivating the soil to produce what it otherwise would not, hybridizing breeds to produce new flowers or fruit—plus the work of building all manner of paraphernalia to support the garden itself, which must be produced from the wood of trees, using tools that must in turn be crafted from ore in the ground.

As for plants, so for mankind. The work of dominion requires planting, cultivating, and raising godly seed. Dominion, to image God, must be fruitful. Thus, God made mankind to be fruitful—and gave the man a biological drive equal to the importance of the task.

Sex, in other words, is the engine of dominion.

3 Sex Is Very Good

THEN THE LORD GOD SAID, "IT IS NOT GOOD
for the man to be alone; I will make him a helper
suitable for him." . . . So the LORD God caused a
deep sleep to fall upon the man, and he slept; then
He took one of his ribs and closed up the flesh at
that place. The LORD God fashioned into a woman the rib which He had taken from the man, and
brought her to the man. The man said,

"This is now bone of my bones,
And flesh of my flesh;
She shall be called Woman,
Because she was taken out of Man."

> For this reason a man shall leave his father and
> his mother, and be joined to his wife; and they
> shall become one flesh. (Gen. 2:18, 21–24)

Sex is the engine of dominion—what does that
mean? It means that the union of male and female
in one flesh drives mankind forward in their created purpose of bringing heaven to earth by establishing God's rule.

While it is easy to think of the two halves of the
creation mandate as being for Adam and Eve re-
spectively, this is not quite right. Adam *is* best fitted to subduing the world, and Eve is best fitted to
filling it. But these duties of dominion fall on them
both, because the creation mandate is given to
mankind collectively. So as the head, the patriarch
Adam is responsible for filling just as much as he is
for subduing.

Mankind's duties to God therefore require the cooperation of the sexes. This, too, is part of God's design, and nowhere is this more obvious than in man's
libido. Just as his aggressive desire to rule and subdue is God-given, so is his powerful desire for sex.
Remember, the dominion God made us for is *fruitful*. Sex is the engine that drives this fruitfulness.

This reality has been difficult for the Church to
accept throughout the ages. Sex is often seen as
dirty in and of itself. There is an earthy animality to
it that is embarrassing to heavenly-minded theolo-
gians—especially ones saturated in the Greek idea

of base flesh and pure spirit. Attitudes like these have moved us toward the modern intuition that women are purer and more pious than men, primarily because their physical appetites are less intense, or less disgusting, if you prefer. Men, we are told, are pigs.

But, believe it or not, the Church probably has a healthier view of sex in *general* today than it did in previous times. In the Victorian era, women were not believed to be capable of orgasm, and any woman who accidentally experienced such a thing was diagnosed to be in the grip of "hysterical paroxysm." And this was the least of the problems that Victorians had with sex. Yet for all that, they did acknowledge the goodness of wives rendering their marital duties to their husbands. Some of the early Church fathers, by contrast, saw sex even *within marriage* as sinful. Although this may seem ridiculous to us, it is important to understand how someone pious and well-versed in Scripture gets there. Unbridled sexual desire is a fire that has burned many. Proverbs 6:26–28 warns, "For the price of a prostitute reduces one to a loaf of bread, and an adulteress hunts for a precious life. Can anyone take fire in his lap and his clothes not be burned? Or can a person walk on hot coals and his feet not be scorched?" (NASB 2020)

Those who fall into the flames of illicit sexual desire will come out charred. They are scarred with shame, and, having their consciences afflicted by lust, they are instinctively wary of sex. Their experience of the degradation of fornication colors their view even of God-honoring sex. It can be difficult for them to imagine how such a force for sin can ever truly be good.

But only the things made to reach the greatest heights can descend to the lowest depths. A man of great wisdom or strength can do far more than a man of little. The question is which way he bends his talents: to God's ways, or to his own. So it is with sex. It is only because it was made as such a force for good, that it can become such a force for evil.

To take an analogy that Scripture itself uses, while the destructive potential for fire is almost without limit, when properly contained and directed it is also one of the most useful forces in creation. Combustion within the engine bay of a car, for instance, can gut it and reduce it to a twisted shell—but combustion within the engine itself produces enough power to drive that car around the world. As the engine fires, a huge amount of useful mechanical energy is produced. At the turn of a key, lifeless hunks of metal are transformed into a growling machine—an extension of its driver, ready to multiply his own speed and endurance and power.

The same is true of a properly harnessed and aimed sex drive. It is an engine that multiplies the productive power of man.

It was God who blessed Adam with a sex drive. He didn't just *command* Adam to be fruitful and multiply. He *designed* him to be so. God could have made mankind's multiplication to be an asexual endeavor. But He didn't. It takes the entangling of two fleshes, of a man and a woman, to make another human life. We are created to produce and reproduce. Thus, it should not be surprising that men are attracted to and aroused by the potential fruitfulness of a woman.

Multiple studies have confirmed the teaching of common sense and Scripture: men are turned on by fertility cues. Listen to the wisdom of Proverbs 5:18–19: "Let your fountain be blessed, and rejoice in the wife of your youth. Like a loving doe and a graceful mountain goat, let her breasts satisfy you at all times; be exhilarated always with her love" (NASB 2020).

Yes and amen. A man is especially aroused by the sway of a woman's hips—they will bring his children into this world. A man is especially aroused by the shape and size of a woman's breasts—they will nurture his children out of infancy. A man is especially aroused by a woman who is ovulating—she can bring forth new life from him. He is aroused by what is smooth, what is tight, what is beautiful—for God has wired us to be fruitful, and these all reflect fruitful youth. Just as God formed and then filled the world with life, so does man desire to take a wife and fill her with life.

One of the great blessings of a man's sex drive is how it urges him to become more than himself. Ultimately, it is not just about having sex, because a man's sexual desire drives him to headship: to become responsible not just for himself, but to take to himself a woman as a wife. One flesh joins with another, and they become a single flesh. From this union, forged in sex, God is pleased to bring forth new flesh: children. What better demonstrates the "one fleshness" of a marriage than the creation of an individual made of those two fleshes? Moreover, this new person magnifies God all the more in that he also bears God's image.

The desire for sex is central to filling the world with the image of God. Our desires—when submitted to God's created order—compel us to extend God's rule, and to fill His world with more image-bearers. The sexes are designed to be productive, to be fruitful, and this fruitfulness requires cooperation. We are made to complement each other to such a degree that the creation mandate is impossible without male *and* female.

Hence, it is not good that a man be alone. He requires a helper suitable to him—a woman. And she needs someone whom she can help. Sexual cooperation is God's design.

But notice one more thing about this design: what it builds. Man and woman are not made to form bonds for merely sentimental reasons, without being fruitful. Union is not the end goal: it is the means to fruitfulness and productivity. But neither are we made to come together merely to produce offspring and then part ways again—as if union were irrelevant. Rather, we are united in the bond of marriage, and this bond exists to establish a community that builds upon itself. The bond expands to encompass more than the original couple; yet rather than reducing them, it instead magnifies them by establishing them at the head of a new community.

This is a glorious point, worth pondering in a world that has normalized cohabitation, divorce, and consumption.

God has precisely calibrated sex to produce *households*. Sex is an engine designed to generate this particular kind of fruitful community, a community that is central in all of life and Scripture. It does not just produce *homes*. It does not just produce *families*. It produces *households*: the total sum of a husband and wife's fruitful work, bound together by covenant love. Alastair Roberts explains it this way:

> The household is bound up with the family. It's something that develops over time. It's a living organism. And it develops through stages. So, a couple gets together and they form a life together. They build a world around themselves. They bear children that they welcome into that world. And they accumulate possessions and influence within the world. In all of these ways, that's the household growing. The household is the realm that is created around the family. The orbit that

it creates around itself through the gravity it as-
serts upon its surroundings.[1]

A household is a miniature world. It is a micro-
cosmos. Every household is one atom in the substance of God's kingdom. And it is through man's
powerful sex drive that these households are built.
Then, through households, societies are established. Culture begins and emanates from the
household. It is where the next generation of men
is shaped and trained, until they leave their father
and mother, join themselves to a wife, and start the
process anew.

It is through households that dominion is exercised. One man alone achieves very little. A man
and wife achieve more. A man, his wife, and their
grown children are a force to be reckoned with—
especially as those children in turn build households that fit together into his, establishing an extended house of considerable resource, influence,
and power.

As households multiply like this, cities are
formed. Soon the relationships of this network of
households must be managed and protected, and
so the natural role of the patriarch is extended into
the office of the magistrate; civil government is

1. "Transcript of a Biblical Theology of Households,"
Adversaria Videos and Podcasts, March 11, 2019,
https://adversariapodcast.com/2019/03/11/transcript-of-a
-biblical-theology-of-the-household.

established. Cities form alliances with other cities and form states. States covenant with other states and form nations. Thus it is that commonwealths, kingdoms, and even great empires spring forth from the natural, God-endowed sex drives of men.

Sex is the engine of God's dominion: the means by which He designed man to establish heaven on earth.

And that is why Satan hates sex.

4 The War on Sex

SATAN HATES SEX. THIS MIGHT SOUND ABSURD to you.

Everything in our culture would have you think otherwise. George Carlin once joked, "The main reason Santa is so jolly is because he knows where all the bad girls live." In the same vein, Woody Allen quipped, "Is sex dirty? Only when it's being done right." The world and its ruler would have us believe that sex is best when it's dirty, best when it's with the bad girls. By natural contrast, then, Christians are fastidious prudes, drawing up from our "puritanical" and Victorian roots an embarrassment about sex, and an ethic that teaches us to be naked and ashamed.

On the face of it, the devil is all about sex; the Church not so much.

As we have mentioned, there is some truth to the Church's ambivalence toward sex. But there is actually *no* truth to the devil's love for it. It only seems this way because he is obsessed with sexual *license*. The devil is for fornication, adultery, and every kind of devious sexual immorality. He loves sex like tin-pot dictators love foreign aid. He hijacks something meant for good and twists it for his own purposes. The foreign aid was meant to buy food to feed a starving people; the tin-pot dictator uses it to buy weapons to subjugate them. Sex was meant to knit two people together and fill the world with more servants of Christ; Satan uses it to alienate people and fill the world with more slaves of lust.

In 1 Corinthians 7, Paul warns married couples not to forgo sex for long, "so that Satan will not tempt you because of your lack of self-control" (v. 5).

Sex, rightly ordered, is unitive and fruitful.

Sex, perverted, is a source of division and barrenness.

The latter is the sort of sex that Satan loves, because the former is the sort that he hates. And his hatred goes far beyond mere intercourse. He hates the whole *system* of biological sex. He hates the whole righteously embodied expression of it that we call gender. He is an enemy of male and female. Why? Because he hates the divine structure of the cosmos. He hates God's kingdom, and the millions of atoms it is built up from: households. In his mind, the only right ruler of heaven and earth is him. There are many hints about this in Scripture, but we see it especially clearly in Revelation 12:7–9:

> And there was war in heaven, Michael and his angels waging war with the dragon. The dragon and his angels waged war, and they were not strong enough, and there was no longer a place found for them in heaven. And the great dragon was thrown down, the serpent of old who is called the devil and Satan, who deceives the whole world; he was thrown down to the earth, and his angels were thrown down with him.

Jonathan Edwards explains that, though he lost the war in heaven, "Satan still hoped to get the victory by subtlety."[1] As we mentioned in the first chapter, sometimes evil patriarchy wages war overtly; sometimes more subtly. When the strong-arm tactics of Pharaoh fail, the devil switches to the covert methods of Absalom. He will use any means he can to destroy God's order and ascend to His throne. Thus, while he attacks overtly in heaven, on earth he pursues a more covert approach. If he cannot flatten hierarchy from the top down, perhaps he can cause it to tumble from the bottom up.

1. Jonathan Edwards, Sermon V in *The Works of Jonathan Edwards*, Vol. 4 (New York: Levitt and Allen, 1852), 148.

Thus he focuses a sneak attack on God's vicegerents, mankind.

His strategy is to divide and conquer. He is a crafty serpent. He knows that if a house is divided against itself, that house will not be able to stand (Mark 3:25). So he seeks to sow confusion and division among mankind.

To understand how he does this, we need to return to Genesis.

We know that God is a God of order and not confusion (1 Cor. 14:33). In Scripture, order means that everything is in its correct place—but also that every place is in its correct *rank*. The fact that God cherishes order in this way is clear in the first chapters of Genesis. It is one of the very first things we learn about Him. When He creates the world from nothing, for a brief time it is "waste and void"—as Calvin puts it, "rude and unpolished, or rather shapeless chaos."[2] Why would He make it this way? To order it—and thus to model for man what his own task will be as God's representative, carrying on dominion in His stead (Gen. 1:26–28). This process of dominion, of forming the world into something "very good," is a process with two halves: dividing and filling:

- God fills the world with light, and divides the light from the darkness. By doing this, He also

2. John Calvin, *Commentaries on the First Book of Moses Called Genesis*, vol. 1, trans. John King (Grand Rapids: Eerdmans, 1948), Gen. 1:2.

divides the cosmos into two fundamental realms: night and day.

- He divides the waters from the waters, establishing two more realms: sea and sky.
- He divides the waters from the land, establishing another realm: the habitable earth.
- He fills the earth with vegetation, divided by kind.
- He fills the sky with luminaries, divided by magnitude.
- He fills the seas and skies with swarms of creatures, divided by kind.
- He fills the earth with beasts, divided by kind.
- He divides man from the earth, and then divides woman from the man.

By the end of this process, the cosmos is no longer rude and unpolished, chaotic and confused. It has been ordered into something pristine and beautiful; something where peace reigns because everything is in its place. God Himself declares that it is very good.

In so doing, He also communicates a foundational principle which underlies the whole process of His dividing and filling: the principle of **telos**. Telos is the end goal, the intended purpose, the aim or design of a thing. It is, in short, what a thing is *for.*

God does everything for a reason. The realms into which He divides the cosmos, and the things with which He fills them, have meaning, because they have purposes that He intends for them when He makes them. They are "very good" not because they are morally upright (only persons can be morally upright), but because they fit very well the purposes for which He made them. They have a telos— and they are perfectly fitted to it.

God's ordering thus goes beyond the mere shaping of chaotic mass into physical harmony. There are unique aesthetic, symbolic, spiritual purposes for each thing He makes. Some of these purposes are revealed; some are not. It isn't important here to trace out, say, the unique telos of light and darkness—or badgers and bull sharks. What is important is to note two things:

1. All creation shares, participates in, and reflects *one* ultimate telos: to serve and bring glory to God. Colossians 1:16–18 says that "all things have been created through Him and for Him . . . so that He Himself will come to have first place in everything." In the same way, Romans 11:36: "For from Him and through Him and to Him are all things. To Him be the glory forever. Amen."
2. Each created thing participates *differently* in this ultimate telos, according to its unique place and design.

In other words, the telos is not etched uniformly onto every created thing, regardless of its shape. It

is not forced upon each thing in the same way, as
if each were the same. It is not imposed in a way
that flattens or blurs or downplays or removes the
distinctions between them. Rather, the overarching telos is *why* those distinctions exist in the first
place. The divisions between things are how God
orders them all toward the ultimate goal of glorifying Him. A creation without distinctions is a world
that is waste and void, formless and empty, chaotic and futile. Creation is not and should not be a
homogeneous mass. It can only glorify God when
everything is in its place—not when all things are
mushed together.

The importance of this is impossible to overes-
timate. To give an analogy, sharing in the common
goal of winning a football game does not eliminate
the distinctions between the players. Rather, it is
why the team is divided into those positions in the
first place. A team with eleven quarterbacks is not a
"very good" team.

By the same token, sharing in the common goal
of producing power does not eliminate the distinctions between the parts of an engine. Rather, this
common purpose is why the engine has parts at all.
If you were to melt everything down into an undifferentiated hunk of metal, it would no longer produce power. It would not be a "very good" engine.

This is true also of bodies (1 Cor. 12:14–26), both
literal and symbolic. A man with a head only, and
no torso or limbs, is hardly a "very good" man. An

army with everyone in command is an army with everyone in confusion. And a house with many heads cannot stand. Vertical divisions are not only as fitting as horizontal ones, but they are also as necessary and indispensable. It is good that all creatures are subordinated beneath their creator. And it is also good that some created things are subordinated beneath others.

Modern evangelicals are quick to defend the importance of God dividing things horizontally. For instance, we ardently defend the goodness of individuality. Each of us by nature thinks of himself as a special snowflake. By the same token, we are happy enough that God created more than two hundred species of finches. But when it comes to acknowledging the significance of His *vertical* divisions, we are reluctant. Man is the glory of God, but woman is the glory of man (1 Cor. 11:7). What a strange saying—who can know it? The Westminster Shorter Catechism speaks of the husband as superior to the wife, and of lay people as inferior to their leaders. How fortunate that we are no longer living in the seventeenth century!

Why do we respond this way? Because we live in a culture that shames rather than glorifies the vertical ways that God divided creation.

But divide He did. The land and the sky are raised above the sea. The sun is a greater light than the moon, ruling over a greater realm (Gen. 1:16). The beasts of the field are stronger than the beasts that creep. Even "star differs from star in glory" (1 Cor. 15:39–41).

In other words, God's ordering of creation by division is not just a separation into kinds, but into hierarchies. Authority and submission, strong and weak, height and depth, holy and common, inner and outer, greater and lesser—these are all built into the structure of the cosmos from the very days of creation . . . and they are all *very good*.

Hence, when God divides the man from the earth, the man is over the earth—and God is over the man. This is the structure of the relationship between God's place, man's place, and the earth's place. And when God divides the woman from the man, the woman is also over the earth, but the man is over the woman. "Christ is the head of every man, and the man is the head of a woman, and God is the head of Christ . . . for indeed man was not created for the woman's sake, but woman for the man's sake" (1 Cor. 11:3, 9). Authority flows downward from God, to Christ, to man, to his wife. When you hear that archaic saying that "a man should know his place"—or, heaven forbid, when someone dares to suggest the same of a woman—you are hearing a statement of God's original design. That statement may or may not be correct in assuming *what* the right place is; but it is entirely correct in assuming *that* both man and woman have a place—and our fellowship, joy, and productivity are found in knowing and keeping it. The Fall itself can be aptly summarized as woman not knowing her place, and man not keeping his.

The corollary of this is that the gospel restores us to our respective places. We have mentioned how grace restores nature: God is working in history to redeem the creation and renew it. His end goal is a world in which the original creation has grown from the original seed into the full glory of a mature tree (cf. 1 Cor. 15:35–37). This begins with the household.

This brings us back to Satan, and his strategy for inverting this natural order. Now, as in the garden, he tempts mankind that we "will be like God." Rather than a direct attack on the head of the hierarchy, he starts at the bottom, with the woman. Attacking the weaker vessel (1 Pet. 3:7), he is able to defeat her not by force but by subtlety—tricking her into doubting the boundaries that God had established. Pay careful attention to the *outcome:* he flattens in her mind the distinction between creator and creation. Her natural action as a result is to eat the fruit, and to get her husband to heed her error and do the same. In this way, she is recruited as Satan's ally to flatten not only the distinction between mankind and God, but further the distinction between woman and man. Following the devil's lead, she inverts the natural hierarchy entirely: God → man → woman → creature becomes creature (serpent) → woman → man → God.

Satan sought to reorganize God's creation: to overturn the hierarchy of God, man, woman, creation. To achieve this, he set a match to the root of the structure. The animals were meant to be subject to the rule of mankind, and yet we find a serpent counseling the woman. The woman was meant to be helper to the man's work of representing God, and yet she encourages him to rebel against God. And Adam, the lord of creation whose wife should have heeded his counsel, instead heeds hers and uses the authority delegated to him to set up his own kingdom instead of God's.

But God is not mocked. His world only works because it is held together by the word of His power (Heb. 1:3). He cannot be replaced. He will not submit to Adam. The fire that Satan uses to burn down the created order cannot touch its creator. For a father to submit to a son, or a king to a prince, or a creator to a creature—this is unnatural. Will the thing molded say to the molder, "Why did you make me thus?" Or will the potter ask advice of the clay?

Man has chosen a life outside of God's rule and order. Although God will eventually restore him to his proper place, the creation structure is upset and overturned. It is fundamentally damaged, and a curse accompanies the promise of redemption. Life outside of God's rule and order is a life cursed with death and difficulty. The harmony between God and mankind is broken because of Adam's rebellion. The fellowship between man and woman is cursed because they inverted it. The very earth pushes against its disgraced rulers. Where previously all the pieces of creation fit together seamlessly, now they are malformed and on edge. Where once the diversity of creation had participated harmoniously in the telos of glorifying God, now it competes against itself. Where originally the world had been unified in its divisions, now it is easily fractured by them.

Satan continues his primordial strategy of turning the sexes against each other—and against God. He loves to sow confusion and division, convincing mankind that life is better outside of God's created order, and that human beings can be redeemed and made perfect apart from their redeemer and perfecter.

Satan does this because it is the only way he can attack God and forestall His complete dominion on the earth. Preventing mankind from fulfilling the creation mandate is the only way the devil can delay his own destruction in the lake of fire.

This is the origin of the "war of the sexes." But it is not the war that you have been taught to notice.

On the surface, it seems obvious that there *is* a war between the sexes. Isn't that what feminists have been saying for generations? Isn't that what all the Men Going Their Own Way are acknowledging? Why would Men's Rights Activists exist if there wasn't a war being waged on manhood by the Feminine Imperative? Doesn't the very ubiquity of the term "toxic masculinity" demonstrate that masculinity is under attack?

All of this is true—yet it is also nothing but confused skirmishing between combatants who themselves are unwitting victims in a far larger conflict: a protracted assault on the very division between the sexes themselves.

The gender war is not *between* the genders. It is *on* the genders. Gender itself is under siege.

Consider Warren Farrell. Although he is widely regarded as the father of the men's movement, he actually advocates that "there should be neither a women's movement blaming men, nor a men's movement blaming women, but a gender liberation movement freeing both sexes from the rigid roles of the past toward more flexible roles for their future."[3] Or, in the pithier words of feminist icon Gloria Steinem, "We need to raise boys more like we raise girls."

Why though?

It's simple: these people rightly see that sexual distinctions are a source of conflict. Absent unity with and through God, the divisions built into creation do divide. Rebelling against God and His order does not eliminate that need for redemption and perfection. And so their solution, to achieve

3. Warren Farrell, interview by Jan Jekieleke, New Tang Dynasty (NTD), March 16, 2021, https://www.ntd.com/dr-warren -farrell-why-bidens-new-gender-policy-council-is-sexist _581853.html.

this redemption and perfection, is to get rid of the source of conflict: to get rid of the sexes themselves.

If we can mush the genders into a homogeneous humanity, there will be no more divisions, no more tensions, no more conflict. And so girls are taught to be more masculine because masculine achievements are the ones that matter; boys to be more feminine because the masculine nature is toxic and disgusting. Contrary to Genesis 1:26–31, they grow up believing that it's not good to be their sex. They therefore have no clue how to live as God designed them.

The enemy of our day is not male versus female (misogyny), or female versus male (misandry). The enemy of our day is androgyny—humanity, spurred on by the devil, versus sexual distinctions.

The devil hates fruitfulness. When the sexes complement and cooperate, the result is a world full of God's image-bearers. As Pharaoh hated the fruitfulness of the Israelites, so Satan hates the fruitfulness of God's image-bearers. He continues to try to wrest dominion from them by harnessing, pacifying, and if necessary destroying man. He will do whatever he can to create barrenness, and he knows that blurring the genders and turning the sexes against each other is a highly effective strategy.

By sowing division between both man and God, and man and woman, Satan undermines the ordering principle of the cosmos: the household. When he divides man from God, he separates the household from its telos: building God's kingdom and establishing His rule on earth. When he divides man from woman, he frustrates the cooperation necessary to construct households in the first place. He wars against the Patriarchy in heaven by warring against the patriarchy down here on earth. It is Satan's dominion versus God's dominion.

5 Spiritual War & Spiritual Worship

THE WAR BETWEEN PATRIARCHIES IS ULTIMATELY spiritual. As you have seen, Absalom and Pharaoh are the enemies of God's people—but they are not our ultimate enemies. They are captains on the earthly battlefield, directed by generals in the spiritual realm. They represent the earthly forces of the evil patriarchy, established at the fall. The serpent is its father, and mankind his brood of vipers. Behind every bad human patriarch stands his spiritual father, Satan, whose desires he does. In the words of A.W. Pink, "The fall has issued in man's becoming the bondslave of Satan. . . . [Holy writ] reveals that men are morally the devil's children (Acts 13:10; I

John 3:10), that they are his captives (2 Tim. 2:26) and under his power (Acts 26:18; Col. 1:13), that they are determined to do what he wants (John 8:44)."[1]

Remember that Satan's chief desire is his own dominion, and his critical strategy in achieving this goal is tearing down God's hierarchy and frustrating the fruitfulness of his image-bearers. Thus, androgyny is a key element in the devil's project.

The heart of this satanic work in the present day is summarized by clinical psychologist and marriage counselor Randi Gunther:

> It became more and more apparent that quality people of both genders would be happier and more fulfilled if they could combine power and nurturing. Men would develop their feminine side and women their masculine. No longer would it be that the bad boys were sexy and the good women were virtuous. Now quality men needed to add chivalry to their power, and women to claim their ability for independent thinking and leadership. They could imagine a relationship where both were equally blended and free to be the best they could be. "She" and "he" became the new idealized "we."[2]

1. A.W. Pink, *Our Accountability to God* (1969; Chicago: Moody Bible Institute, 1999), 134.

2. Randi Gunther, "Why Great Husbands Are Being Abandoned," *Huffington Post*, October 13, 2014, https://www.huffpost.com/entry/marriage-advice_b_5666990.

This project has been ongoing for generations now, and as Randi says, it has produced a great many men who are "the androgynous guys that their women have asked them to become." But, Randi explains, this project hasn't ended as anticipated:

You would think that the women in these new relationships would be ecstatic . . . Well, guess again. Fifty percent of marriages are still ending in divorce, and women continue to be the gender that initiates those endings. In the past, their reasons for leaving most often had to do with infidelity, neglect, or abuse. Now they're dumping men who are faithful, attentive, and respectful, the very men they said they have always wanted. Why would women who have accomplished the female dream suddenly not be satisfied with it? Why are they leaving these ideal guys, and for what reasons?

I am currently dealing with several of these great husbands. They are, across the board, respectful, quality, caring, devoted, cherishing, authentic, and supportive guys whose wives have left them for a different kind of man.

You may think that these women are ruthless and inconsiderate. Those I know are far from that. More often, they still love their husbands as much as they ever did, but in a different way. They tell me how wonderful their men are and how much they respect them. They just don't want to be married to them anymore.

The women I have treated who have left their husbands for more "masculine" men believed that their new relationships would be able to both excite and nurture them. Sadly, that has not always happened. The veritable saint with balls is as elusive as ever.[3]

Note Randi's scare quotes around "masculine"—she still believes that androgyny is ideal because she is religiously committed to it. She writes an article documenting how destructive androgyny is to marriage and concludes that couples must simply figure out a way to make androgyny work. Of course, she herself, a psychologist and marriage counselor, has not the slightest idea how to make her ideal work. But she cannot consider any other option, because that would be misogynistic and toxic.

Or, to put it into a more ancient vernacular, it would be heretical and blasphemous.

We are not exaggerating or trying to sensationalize. The war between the patriarchies, the war on gender, is *spiritual* in nature. Anyone who has observed this war, let alone fought in it, knows that the commitment to androgynism is religious. It is not scientific. Every element—from the madness of transgenderism to women in combat—works against the natural structures of creation.

Dr. Peter Jones has ably documented that androgyny is a recurring and persistent pattern in pagan

3. Gunther, "Why Great Husbands Are Being Abandoned."

mythology throughout history—and actually constitutes the pagan sexual ideal. Sociologically, pagan cultures uphold the created order, out of practical necessity. But spiritually, they upend it, out of *religious* necessity. From the Sumerian cult of Ishtar with its sexually ambiguous priests, to the cult of Bacchus with its initiation by homosexual rape, to the literally emasculated priests of Cybele, to the homosexual pederasty of famous theosophists, paganism produces and glories in ritualized androgyny.

This is inevitable. Androgyny is a foundational doctrine of paganism.

Why? Because God is just, and His justice is both consistent and wise. When people sin, therefore, He will always judge them; and when He judges them, His punishments always fit their crimes. When He curses sin, He does not do so randomly or haphazardly but rather in keeping with the transgression. For instance, Adam was made by God to keep the earth; when he rebelled against God, the earth was cursed to rebel against him. Eve was made by God to help Adam rule and reproduce; when she rebelled, she was cursed with a rebellious spirit against Adam's rulership and pain in reproducing. Satan was made to have authority in the heavenly places; when he rebelled by trying to get power in the earthly places, attacking its weaker ruler (the woman), he was cursed by being made lower than the earthly beasts and being promised death at the hands of the woman's seed.

And so in the same way, Romans 1:18–27 tells us that when men exchange the glory of the immortal God for images of created things, God also puts them under a specific curse fitted to their sin:

> For they exchanged the truth of God for a lie, and worshiped and served the creature rather than the Creator, who is blessed forever, amen. For this reason God gave them over to degrading passions; for their women exchanged the natural function for that which is unnatural, and in the same way also the men abandoned the natural function of the woman and burned in their desire toward one another, men with men committing indecent acts and receiving in their own persons the due penalty of their error. (vv. 25–27)

Ritual androgyny, typified in sodomy, is the sacrament of paganism. There is a logical connection between exchanging the worship of God for the worship of creation and the vilest forms of effeminacy and butchness. This connection is easily understood when we think about what man is: the image of God. This is not a random description unconnected from the rest of the world man was placed in to rule over. It illustrates a key principle found everywhere in the Bible: that the physical images the spiritual. Everything seen is a representation of something unseen. In *The Story of Sex and Scripture*, Bill Mouser notes that God is not anthropomorphic; rather, creation is theomorphic.[4] Man is the image of God; yet also, male and female are an image of the creator and creation. What God does in creating Eve from Adam is a microcosm of what He had already done in creating the world. The world came from Him, is distinct from Him, and has the purpose of union with Him. Eve came from Adam, is distinct from him, and has the purpose of union with him. Paul makes this point explicitly in Ephesians 5:31–32. There, he narrows it down to speak specifically of the Church, but when we compare Colossians 1:16–20, Romans 8:20–23, and Genesis 9:9–17, we see that while the Church is the pinnacle of God's intention, He extends this design to creation more generally.

In other words, the principle of male and female doesn't originate in Adam and Eve, but in God and creation.

So what should we *expect* to happen when man consciously rejects this hierarchy? What happens when he denies the distinction between God and creation?

He continues to follow the devil in confusing, denying, and ultimately trying to obliterate the *image* of that divide. He starts to sacralize androgyny. The devil loves and encourages paganism because it overturns the creation order he hated from the

4. William E. and Barbara K. Mouser, *The Story of Sex in Scripture* (Waxahachie, TX: International Council for Gender Studies, 2006), 13.

beginning, affording his best chance to swap places with God (cf. Is. 14:12–14). Paganism is Satan's religion. He loves and encourages androgyny because he understands its religious significance. As Jones puts it:

> The physico-theological mechanism seems to function as follows: androgynous persons, whether homosexual or bi-sexual, are able to express within themselves both sexual roles and identities. In the sex act they engage both as male and female, equally as penetrator and penetrated, the "hard" and the "soft"—and thus taste in some form or other both physical and spiritual androgyny. As in classic monistic spirituality, they have, on the physical plane, joined the opposites, proving and experiencing that there are no distinctions. Just as the distinctions inherent in heterosexuality point to the fundamental theistic notion of the Creator/creature distinction, so androgyny in its various forms eradicates distinction and elevates the spiritual blending of all things, including the idolatrous confusion of the human with the divine. This seems to be the very same logic that brings Paul to a similar conclusion already in Romans 1:18–27. . . .

Clearly God is interested in sex, or Satan would not be so passionately committed to its deconstruction. To destroy God's created structures, the Evil One rips from the body politic the sexual distinctions hard-wired into creation to recall the deep truth about existence—the absolute distinction between the Creator and creation.[5]

Modern secular androgyny is just one more variant on pagan thinking—the spiritual mindset that Paul speaks of in Romans 1:18ff. It is found in any worldview that collapses the creator/creature distinction, the essence of Satan's desire. You cannot collapse this distinction without further collapsing all the other distinctions that depend upon it.

Contrary to the popular saying, "I'm spiritual but not religious," Scripture teaches us that *every* man is *inherently* religious. He might not have a *religion*, with clear doctrines and overt rituals, but he is nonetheless *religious,* engaging in worship. Religiousness starts in the heart, where God has placed eternity (Eccles. 3:11). Whether or not it overflows into the development of orthodoxy or orthopraxy, man remains in every way very religious, because God made him for a religious purpose: to serve his creator.

In the modern age, where individualism is the name of the game, paganism does not show up in religions so much as in religiousness. People are often irreligious, eschewing religion, but they are never unreligious, worshipping no god. This is veiled

5. Peter Jones, "Androgyny: The Pagan Sexual Ideal," *Journal of the Evangelical Theological Society,* 43, no. 3 (September 2000): 443–69.

because we have come to associate worship with certain kinds of beliefs and rituals: religions. But the Bible does not have such a narrow view. It does not confine worship to doctrine and ritual. Rather, it defines worship primarily in terms of *service*.

This is because service is what man was created for—to do that which God requires of him. This extends far beyond performing rituals in certain times and places, which is why the stock phraseology throughout Deuteronomy parallels serving and worshipping:

> It shall come about if you ever forget the LORD your God and go after other gods and serve them and worship them, I testify against you today that you will surely perish. . . .
>
> Beware that your hearts are not deceived, and that you do not turn away and serve other gods and worship them. . . .
>
> If there is found in your midst, in any of your towns, which the LORD your God is giving you, a man or a woman who does what is evil in the sight of the LORD your God, by transgressing His covenant, and has gone and served other gods and worshiped them, or the sun or the moon or any of the heavenly host, which I have not commanded. . . .
>
> They went and served other gods and worshiped them, gods whom they have not known and whom He had not allotted to them. . . .

But if your heart turns away and you will not obey, but are drawn away and worship other gods and serve them. . . . (Deut. 8:19; 11:16; 17:2–3; 29:26; 30:17)

Similar phrasing in places like Exodus 32:8 also parallels sacrificing and worshipping or obeying and worshipping (1 Kings 11:33; 2 Chron. 7:19). It is through our *service* that we are supposed to glorify and enjoy God forever (cf. Ps. 29:2; 99:5; Rom.12:1; Jas. 1:27).

This is built into us; we can't not do it, just as a clock can't not display a time. If we reject God, we don't stop doing what He made us to do; we simply do it wrong. We can tell the wrong time, but we can't tell no time at all. Even in our fallen state, we are unwittingly groping for God (Acts 17:22, 26). So if we refuse to glorify and serve and enjoy Him, we automatically will be glorifying and serving and enjoying something else.

This is all worship.

To put this in the simplest terms, the Bible doesn't just treat worship as something done on your knees. It is first and foremost something done on your feet. Doing obeisance is merely a physical image of one's larger service to one's god. For Christians, this looks like Romans 12:1 and James 1:27: "Therefore I urge you, brethren, by the mercies of God, to present your bodies a living and holy sacrifice, acceptable to God, which is your spiritual service of worship"; "Pure and undefiled religion in the sight of our God and Father is this: to visit orphans and widows in their distress, and to keep oneself unstained by the world."

The corollary is that, for non-Christians, it looks like whatever they do instead. Jesus's words in Matthew 25:44–46 are apropos:

> Then they themselves also will answer, "Lord, when did we see You hungry, or thirsty, or a stranger, or naked, or sick, or in prison, and did not take care of You?" Then He will answer them, "Truly I say to you, to the extent that you did not do it to one of the least of these, you did not do it to Me." These will go away into eternal punishment, but the righteous into eternal life.

Although it is easy to think that people who don't engage in religious ritual are not worshipping, this is contrary to how religion and worship works according to Scripture. Paul tells us that greed is idolatry (Col. 3:5)—and we know that idolatry is worship. So, do you know any people who eschew overtly religious rituals, yet spend their days in service of mammon, coveting some new purchase or some new experience? What are they serving? What are they glorifying? What are they enjoying? Answer those questions, and you will also discover what (and how) they are worshipping. It is not that deep down, such people—who truly don't think about religion—actually have secret pagan beliefs. Rather, it is that, right on the surface, they have exchanged the glory of God for the creation, and that God Himself tells us how He curses them in a consistent, logical way, by giving them over to certain kinds of depravity. This depravity specifically includes imaging their religious error through their physical bodies.

To explain it from another angle, G.K. Beale famously drew attention to the Bible's presupposition that you become what you worship and that what you revere will be what you resemble:[6]

> Their idols are silver and gold,
> The work of man's hands.
> They have mouths, but they cannot speak;
> They have eyes, but they cannot see;
> They have ears, but they cannot hear;
> They have noses, but they cannot smell;
> They have hands, but they cannot feel;
> They have feet, but they cannot walk;
> They cannot make a sound with their throat.
> Those who make them will become like them,
> Everyone who trusts in them. (Ps. 115:4–8; cf. 2
>   Cor. 3:18; 1 John 3:2)

As Doug Wilson observes in his "Sexual by Design" lecture series, "You can't believe that ultimate reality is infinitely malleable and not think

6. G.K. Beale, *We Become What We Worship: A Biblical Theology of Idolatry* (Downer's Grove, IL: IVP, 2008).

that you have the right within your particular subset of that world to morph and shift and reinvent however it suits you."[7] And how it suits you will look like the work of your father the devil: rebellion against God, expressed through rebellion against His created distinctions. Man will always try to exercise dominion by serving and worshipping a spiritual father.

He cannot help it; it is his nature. The only question is whose dominion it will be. Who will he serve and worship? The choice is stark: serve God to bring heaven to earth—or serve Satan to bring hell.

7. Douglas Wilson, "Sexual by Design, Part 1" (lecture sponsored by Clearnote Church at Indiana University, Bloomington, IL, April 13, 2012), Canon Press. YouTube video, 19:28, https://youtu.be/-ZotiSgc3fI.

6 Toxic Sexuality

MEN ARE ALWAYS REPRESENTING, IMAGING, trusting, worshipping, serving someone. Thus we are always glorifying someone, always seeking to magnify their name. That name is either our own—and thus, indirectly, the devil's—or it is God's.

Since the fall, those serving God have been at constant war with those serving Satan. Their goals and priorities are mutually incompatible. To serve God is to seek to raise up His name and kingdom, to put to death the works of the flesh, and to destroy the works of the devil. By contrast, to serve Satan is to seek to tear down the name and kingdom of God and replace it with murder and lies. This world ain't big enough for two gods.

The struggle for the cosmos, waged between these two lines of descent, these two patriarchies, began with Adam's first two sons. Cain and Abel are seeds for the two houses that still battle today. Understanding this is critical to understanding our own place on the battlefield, and the correct strategy for our spiritual warfare. The characters of Adam's sons will, in one way or another, come to be the distinctive archetypes of their respective lineages. The older brother represents the evil, rebellious, and self-satisfying ways of the serpent—those who corrupt God's way to magnify their own names, and respond in outrage when God is unimpressed. The younger brother represents the pious, obedient, and mission-centered way of life—those who approach God on His own terms and seek to magnify His name: "By faith Abel offered to God a better sacrifice than Cain, through which he obtained the testimony that he was righteous" (Heb. 11:4). "But for Cain and for his offering He had no regard. So Cain became very angry and his countenance fell" (Gen. 4:5).

Their differing orientations toward God will always bring these two seeds into conflict, and the intensity of the struggle is made immediately evident as Cain murders his brother. But Yahweh sustains the godly line with the birth of Seth (Gen. 4:8, 26).

Generally, genealogies exist in Scripture to show how God is moving forward His purpose in a specific family line. But the very first genealogy in the Bible exists to show the opposite: how the house of man looks as it grows apart from the telos of God. The genealogy from Cain to Lamech in Genesis 4:17–22 is bookended by two parallel stories: Cain's murder of Abel, and an intensification of this original event in Lamech's murder of a youth (vv. 9–16; 23–24). Taken as a whole, this genealogy, surrounded by these two stories, reveals three key insights about how the creation mandate is twisted by wicked men.

First, we see that man is still wired to *fulfill* the creation mandate—to exercise dominion and extend rulership into the world. Cain's line is culturally innovative. Cain himself builds a city, and his descendants are credited with the creation of both musical instruments and forged metal tools. They rapidly acquire a command of their world, learning how to bend it to their will. But whose dominion and rulership do they represent? Who do they glorify? It is not the God who made them. They labor not to magnify Yahweh's name and law in creation but rather their own.

This is the foundation on which all wicked patriarchy rests: the intent, following Satan, to make our own name great and to rule as our own hearts desire—as if we exist for ourselves, and from ourselves. It is, ultimately, self-idolatry: the elevation of man to the place of God.

The significance of this can be seen in how un-godly patriarchs build cities as monuments to themselves. Genesis 4 is the first time we see a city, and it is built by Cain—and he "called the name of the city Enoch, after the name of his son" (Gen. 4:17). This city functions as a kind of prototype for Babel in Genesis 11. Notice the same language of making a name: "They said, 'Come, let us build for ourselves a city, and a tower whose top will reach into heaven, and let us make for ourselves a name, otherwise we will be scattered abroad over the face of the whole earth'" (Gen. 11:4).

Babel later becomes Babylon in the time of Israel, and it is recapitulated as a symbolic archetype throughout Scripture. This archetype reaches its cli-max in Revelation 17, where it represents all of the cosmopolitan sophistication and urbane magnifi-cence of worldly culture. As Graeme Goldsworthy notes, "Cities come to figure prominently in the Bible as the expression of human wickedness," glorifying the name of their builders, instead of the name of God Most High.[1] They are an über-house, a mini-kingdom in competition with the kingdom of God. Although they are not *automatically* wicked, they are none-theless a natural expression of mankind's galloping dominion, untethered from God. They arise quickly from the seed of the serpent, because sin is always

---

1. Graeme Goldsworthy, *According to the Plan: The Unfolding of the Revelation of God in the Bible* (Downer's Grove, IL: IVP, 1991), 108.

in a hurry; they arise slowly from the seed of Eve, because God patiently instructs His people in order to lead them into righteousness (cf. Gal. 4:1–5).

The second insight revealed in Genesis 4 is that man's aggressive instinct to rule is twisted into violent tyranny. As Stephen Dempster points out, the genealogy "begins with Cain, the brother-killer, and ends with the child-killer, Lamech."[2] The violence of man was meant to be a tool used to domesticate the wild into a nursery and shelter for God's image-bearers. Now it has become a weapon to eliminate the divine image in man when it threatens the sovereignty or honor of the wicked patriarch.

Third, we see sex and the marriage bed quickly corrupted. God put forth a prototype in Adam and Eve of one woman for one man. The way he created man was not happenstance; it was instruction (cf. Matt. 19:4–9). But in Genesis 4, we find the drive to be fruitful being twisted, as Lamech takes multiple wives. This is only the beginning of the wicked character that becomes magnified in the lives of Cain's descendants. As sin grows, society under an evil patriarchy rapidly deteriorates into what we can rightly call "toxic sexuality."

Such was the case just before God cleansed the world in the flood. In Genesis 6, the sin-defiled strength of the seed of the serpent is combined with the beauty of women to produce a hellish society.

2. Stephen Dempster, *Dominion and Dynasty: A Theology of the Hebrew Bible* (Downer's Grove: IVP, 2003), 70.

How bad is it? God says:

> Then the LORD saw that the wickedness of man
> was great in the earth, and that every intent of the
> thoughts of his heart was only evil continually. And
> the LORD was sorry that He had made man on the
> earth, and He was grieved in His heart. So the LORD
> said, "I will destroy man whom I have created from
> the face of the earth, both man and beast, creeping
> thing and birds of the air, for I am sorry that I have
> made them" . . . Now the earth was corrupt in the
> sight of God, and the earth was filled with violence.
> God looked on the earth, and behold, it was cor-
> rupt; for all flesh had corrupted their way upon the
> earth. (Gen. 6:5–7; 11–12, NKJV).

Satan's sons have finally achieved what the serpent set out to do in Eden: have man destroyed
from the earth. God thwarted this effort early on by
showing mercy to Adam and Eve instead of execut-
ing them. But now, ten generations later, the line of
Adam is so corrupted that God determines it must
indeed be destroyed.

But Noah found grace in His eyes (Gen. 6:8).

Can you see parallels to the modern day? Do we
see today men seeking to make their own names
great? Do we see violence and tyranny? Do we see
sexual perversion and the corruption of marriage?
Of course. These are the times we live in. This is
true "toxic masculinity." It consists in the spiritual

condition we have just been describing. Toxic masculinity is what you find in the sons of the devil.

But the serpent has daughters too.

Toxic sexuality exists for both sexes. In both cases, it takes the form of a spiritual subversion of God's design. So just as there really is toxic masculinity—wicked patriarchy—there is also toxic femininity. The creation mandate was for both sexes; thus, as it is subverted by men in the fall, so it is subverted by women. In both cases the subversion is along sexual lines. There are sins common to men, and there are sins common to women.

Talking about toxic femininity is verboten in evangelicalism. This is why so many men are unprepared for toxic femininity, and why it has become such a potent accelerant of chaos in the modern day. Satan is only too pleased to use the power of female sexuality to magnify the disorder he can cause in the world. But this, too, is nothing new. Apostasy through marriage was the catalyst for the Flood—and for the calamitous fracture of the kingdom of Israel:

> For when Solomon was old, his wives turned his heart away after other gods; and his heart was not wholly devoted to the LORD his God, as the heart of David his father had been. . . . So the LORD said to Solomon, 'Because you have done this, and you have not kept My covenant and My statutes, which I have commanded you, I will surely tear

the kingdom from you, and will give it to your servant." (1 Kings 11:4, 11)

In Proverbs 6:26, Solomon describes an adulteress as a sexual predator, hunting for a precious life.
In 7:26, he warns, "all her slain are a mighty throng"
(ESV). Whereas admonishments about immoral
women are these days shouted down as the bab-
ble of bitter men, Scripture contains the words of
the Holy Spirit. We do well to heed His warnings,
because without wisdom to guide us, the powerful
engine of our sexuality can easily drive us off a cliff.
The danger of immoral women to God's sons is la-
boriously repeated throughout the history of Israel.
When men reject the faith and make shipwrecks of
their lives, it is often because they followed women
who worship other gods.

This same danger compelled the patriarchs to
take great care in finding appropriate wives for
their firstborn sons. Abraham was so adamant that
Isaac would not take a wife "from the daughters of
the Canaanites" that he required his most trusted
servant to travel to his kindred so as to find a woman there (Gen. 24:1–9). The same concern preoc-
cupied Isaac and Rebekah as they considered the
future wife of Jacob. Isaac commanded his son saying, "You must not take a wife from the Canaanite
women" (Gen. 28:1).

In Proverbs, we find both a wise father and a
wise mother warning their son the king about the

dangers of immoral women. In chapters 5 and 7, the father gives two very detailed warnings about the ruin that comes from being caught in the web of a "strange woman." In chapter 31, the mother warns of the strength-depleting nature of promiscuous women (v. 3). These are the daughters whose father is the devil.

In 1 Corinthians 15:33, Paul warns, "Do not be deceived: 'Bad company corrupts good morals.'" What do you think the effects will be of keeping company with a bad wife? A good woman will further your mission of establishing a godly household; a foolish woman "tears it down with her own hands" (Prov. 14:1). Just as a woman must be careful in accepting a proposal of marriage, so must a man be careful in extending one. The consequences of a wise choice are glorious; the consequences of a bad one are dire. "For many are the victims she has cast down and numerous are all her slain. Her house is the way to Sheol, descending to the chambers of death" (Prov. 7:26–27). Many men can testify to the hell it is to be married to an ungodly woman. The best path is always to avoid her altogether. Wisdom says, "Do not stray into her paths" (v. 25).

Satan is eager to harness, pacify, and destroy God's sons, by using his own daughters as bait. Just as he used Eve against Adam, he continues to use toxic femininity as a key pillar in his strategy for inverting the creation order.

You might think you are too smart for that to work on you. Don't be so sure. It has worked on millions of smart men so far. Are you wiser than Solomon? Just because you know how to avoid harlots and hussies doesn't mean you know how to avoid Satan's daughters. The obvious traps are not just there to trap the simple. They are there to distract the wise from the more subtle traps in store. We did not reach our current cultural moment, where evil is accepted, celebrated, and glorified, by *starting* there. We started with covert evil—evil that was subtle and caught men like you unawares. The serpent's children are crafty like he is; they do not advertise what they are—until it is too late. Satan disguises himself as an angel of light (2 Cor. 11:14), and his servants likewise are masters of camouflage. Remember how Jezebel used subterfuge to murder Naboth (1 Kings 21).

Satan has had great success in undercutting the Church's teaching on sexuality, precisely because he has used subtle and covert forms of sexual immorality to compromise her for generations. A central pillar of this strategy is feminine immorality in the form of immodesty.

Here is what we mean:

Harlotry in the Church is rampant today. Yoga pants, short skirts, Daisy Dukes, low-cut tops, caked-on makeup, and the like are obvious and egregious forms of immodesty that go unmentioned and unchallenged in Churches across the Western world.

How did we get to such a low point? It was through the toleration and acceptance of more subtle forms of immodesty that served as the sharp end of the wedge—immodesty characterized not through dress, but through words and deeds: "She is loud and stubborn; her feet abide not in her house" (Prov. 7:11, KJV).

This is the kind of woman whom Satan has deployed en masse to reduce our society to an ash heap. Combined with soft men, she is a highly effective agent of chaos, serving his purpose of inverting the creation order. The loud woman is one who has embraced the curse against Eve to desire her own way: "Your desire shall be contrary to your husband, but he shall rule over you" (Gen. 3:16, ESV) .

This woman is not necessarily one who speaks with too much *volume*. That is only the most crude kind of loudness. The fundamental problem is a loud *heart*. The Hebrew word refers to boisterousness or tumultuousness, turbulence and commotion. It is meant to bring to mind the roaring wind of a storm. Therein we find a good metaphor for her—like a storm, she is full of unruly energy. She yields only to her own passions. She is immodest because she has no sense of "the imperishable quality of a gentle and quiet spirit, which is precious in the sight of God" (1 Pet. 3:4).

Due to the fall, men are prone to passivity—yet are *supposed* to actively take the lead. Women, by contrast, are cursed to want to play the man but are *supposed* to be quiet and deferent. Consider the pattern laid out by Paul:

> Likewise, I want women to adorn themselves with proper clothing, modestly and discreetly, not with braided hair and gold or pearls or costly garments, but rather by means of good works, as is proper for women making a claim to godliness. A woman must quietly receive instruction with entire submissiveness. But I do not allow a woman to teach or exercise authority over a man, but to remain quiet. For it was Adam who was first created, and then Eve. And it was not Adam who was deceived, but the woman being deceived, fell into transgression. But women will be preserved through the bearing of children if they continue in faith and love and sanctity with self-restraint. (1 Tim. 2:9–15)

Evangelicals tend to give all their attention to the explicitly offensive parts of this passage—the ones that require the most apology to feminists. They fail to notice the broader implicit pattern established throughout, which is even *more* offensive to modern sensibilities: that women in the Church are not to draw attention to themselves in any way. They are not to seek to stand over others, whether through their clothing or their speech or their will. Rather, they are to remain meek and modest, quiet and self-restrained, "entirely submissive." This is the very opposite of the modern concern about how to ensure that women are "heard" and "have a voice" in the Church.

The loud woman despises this estate for which God made her. In the hierarchy of creation, she does not know her place. Her loudness and stubbornness lead her away from her household: "her feet do not remain at home" (Prov. 7:11). Though she has a husband, and she is supposed to be submitted to his mission, she refuses. It is his home she should be caught up in the work of building, yet she is off doing her own thing. She will not be "chained down" to the home of one man.

Matthew Henry put it well:

By her place, not her own house; she hates the confinement and employment of that; her feet abide not there any longer than needs must. She is all for gadding abroad, changing place and company. Now is she without in the country, under pretense of taking the air, now in the streets of the city, under pretense of seeing how the market goes. She is here, and there, and every where but where she should be. She lies in wait at every corner, to pick up such as she can make a prey of. Virtue is a penance to those to whom home is a prison.[3]

3. Matthew Henry, *An Exposition of the Old Testament*, vol. 3, *Containing Job, Psalms, Proverbs, and Song of Songs* (Edinburgh: C. Wright, 1758), 456.

Satan loves the loud woman. Well, he loves to *use* her. She hates the household as much as he does, because it represents submission to a will besides her own. Satan is eager to deploy her to prowl for fools.

Commenting on Proverbs 7:10 in their excellent Old Testament commentary, Keil and Delitzsch explain the motives of this brazen woman: that "she is of a hidden mind, of a concealed nature; for she feigns fidelity to her husband and flatters her paramours as her only beloved, while in truth she loves none, and each of them is to her only a means to an end, viz., to the indulgence of her worldly sensual desire."[4]

The loud woman swings from man to man like a monkey swings from branch to branch. Men exist to serve her mission. They are useful insomuch as they allow her to fulfill her desires. Sheryl Sandberg, the COO of Facebook, is a great example of a loud woman—a paradigm of the feminist ideal. In her book *Lean In*, she writes:

> When looking for a life partner, my advice to women is date all of them: the bad boys, the cool boys, the commitment-phobic boys, the crazy boys. But do not marry them. The things that make the bad boys sexy do not make them good husbands.

4. Karl Friedrich Keil and Franz Delitzsch, *Biblical Commentary on the Old Testament, Biblical Commentary on the Proverbs of Solomon, vol. 1* (Edinburgh: T&T Clark, 1874), 101.

When it comes time to settle down, find someone who wants an equal partner. Someone who thinks women should be smart, opinionated, and ambitious. Someone who values fairness and expects or, even better, wants to do his share in the home. These men exist and, trust me, over time, nothing is sexier.[5]

What makes a good husband according to Sandberg? It is a man who does not get in the way of his wife's ambitions. This is why the commanding "alpha males" of her youth won't do. They'll buck against her demands and manipulations. Sandberg, like all loud women, eventually settles on a compliant "beta" who knows who really wears the pants.

This is what makes loud women such bad news. They invert the biblical pattern for the household. Manhood is ultimately about a man building God's house by building his own. This is his spiritual worship. This work can't be completed alone. It requires a woman. Hence, God brought Eve to Adam as a helper to this service. He is the head; she is his body. He is the leader; she is the follower. He is commissioned; she is in submission. He is the glory of God; she is the glory of man. A loud woman, however, will not submit herself to such a situation. It grates against her. She will not stand for masculine

5. Sheryl Sandberg, *Lean In: Women, Work, and the Will to Lead* (New York: Random House, 2013), 115.

rulership. She is not content with her place in God's hierarchy, and she hates the masculine strength that would keep her there.

This is the feminine version of Cain's self-worship that we see in Genesis 4. The loud woman will not center her life on God's glory; it must be her or nothing.

In time, such a woman *will* start seeking her own glory, will start trying to build her own name—and in so doing, she will tear down her house with her own hands (Prov. 14:1). The created order will always, eventually, spin out of control when it is not centered on the glory of God. As goes the household, so goes society—fill a nation with such women, and they will tear down their very civilization.

Fill a church with them, and they will tear down God's house too.

7 The Church Effeminate

THE CHURCH IS THE HOUSEHOLD OF GOD (1 Tim. 3:15). It is the place most focused on serving Him and magnifying His name. It is a spiritual family fathered by the heavenly Patriarch. Jesus Christ, the second person of the Trinity, is Himself a man. Paul, commissioned by Christ, commands Christians to "be on the alert, stand firm in the faith, act like men, be strong" (1 Cor. 16:13). Churches should be places where effeminate men are nurtured into godly manhood, as grace restores their masculine natures. The Church, of all places, should not just welcome patriarchy—the rule of fathers to magnify the name of the Father—but celebrate, cultivate, and teach it.

Today, nothing could be further from the truth. Modern Christian men are faced with an impossible dilemma: lay aside their masculinity or lay aside Christianity. In large numbers, they have chosen the latter.

There should be no conflict between church and manhood, but there is. The Western Church is overwhelmingly comprised of women—of both sexes.

This conflict is primarily rooted in the Church's rejection of the biblical doctrine of anthropology—the nature of man. Christian men today are asked to see themselves as androgynous spirits, trapped in bodies that, unlike women's, have nasty, sinful urges.

But to understand how we got to this point, we need to first understand how such aberrant theology becomes accepted. It starts with simple numbers. As Leon Podles documents in *The Church Impotent*,[1] we have had a problem with male membership for centuries. Most churches' numbers have skewed northward of 60 percent women for many generations. A major reason for this is that the men in the pulpit have been recognized even since the Regency period as "fops." Spurgeon noted this in his day too, and warned his students against it:

1. Leon J. Podles, *The Church Impotent: The Feminization of Christianity*, available at https://www.podles.org/church -impotent.htm.

There are silly young ladies who are in raptures with a dear young man whose main thought is his precious person; these, it is to be hoped, are becoming fewer every day: but as for sensible men, and especially the sturdy workmen of our great cities, they utterly abhor foppery in a minister. Wherever you see affectation you find at once a barrier between that man and the commonsense multitude. Few ears are delighted with the voices of peacocks. It is a pity that we cannot persuade all ministers to be men, for it is hard to see how otherwise they will be truly men of God. It is equally to be deplored that we cannot induce preachers to speak and gesticulate like other sensible persons, for it is impossible that they should grasp the masses till they do. All foreign matters of attitude, tone, or dress are barricades between us and the people: we must talk like men if we would win men.[2]

Spurgeon puts his finger on the chief problem with these preachers: their peculiar kind of vanity. These are men whose identities are bound up with what silly young women think—or sometimes foolish old ones (cf. 2 Tim. 3:6). They are dependent upon female approval for their sense of self-worth and self-security. They are the stereotypical "white knight."

2. Charles Spurgeon, *Lectures to My Students* (1875; Moscow, ID: Canon Press, 2020), 417–18.

A "white knight" is a kind of "nice guy"—one who derives his value specifically from defending damsels in distress from dragons. White knights are willing to engage in a fantasy to achieve this—imagining evil women to be damsels, and good men to be dragons. As secular psychologist Robert Glover puts it in *No More Mr. Nice Guy*, "Just about everything a Nice Guy does is consciously or unconsciously calculated to gain someone's approval or to avoid disapproval."[3] For a white knight, that someone is usually a woman. His desire for female validation is often pursued irrespective of a woman's character, because he assumes that women are of a higher and purer spiritual nature than men. If you ask him in what ways women especially sin that men don't, he will seldom have an answer—but often be scandalized by the question.

The effect that white-knight pastors have on "men's men" has been ably summarized by Spurgeon above—they will not talk like men, and so they will not win men. Thus they have repelled manly men from their pews. But they have also simultaneously enabled influential women to lead their churches into error.

Let's unpack this interplay between white knights and influential women in Western churches because the problem is so ubiquitous and so

---

3. Robert Glover, *No More Mr. Nice Guy: A Proven Plan for Getting What You Want in Love, Sex, and Life* (Philadelphia: Running Press, 2001), 6.

perilous to any man who would happily read a book like this.

When women hold power in a church—whether officially or unofficially—two things tend to happen:

1. They strive to include anyone agreeable, regardless of error.
2. They strive to exclude anyone disagreeable, regardless of orthodoxy.

The reason for this is not due to some defect in women; on the contrary, it is exactly because God designed them to be the knitters-together of a society. Comity and harmony are women's forte, and their ability to influence others toward such togetherness is both good and glorious—in its proper context. If you think of "polite society" at its best, of the way that it tempers the hard edges of men, and establishes a structured space in which everyone can be included and feel confident of a place through observing the proper decorum, this is largely driven by feminine virtues. However, without masculine rulership it easily turns grotesque and pathological, with subtle hierarchies and cliques and unspoken rules that exclude anyone deemed offensive.

Women will always be tempted to remove discomfort. This happens even with the best women, out of a well-intentioned concern for the emotional well-being of others. It happens even more with the worst women, where it is motivated by selfish emotional inertia and conflict avoidance. Either way, biblical Christianity requires *discomfort* because it requires *discipline:* "All discipline for the moment seems not to be joyful, but sorrowful; yet to those who have been trained by it, afterwards it yields the peaceful fruit of righteousness" (Heb. 12:11).

Temporary pain at the hands of "church fathers" yields the lasting peaceful fruit of righteousness. Men who faithfully imitate Jesus, the prophets, and the apostles, are therefore both proficient at ruffling feathers and likely to do so. This directly rubs against the grain of women's instincts.

By contrast, however, false teachers are experts at being agreeable. This goes back to Eden, when the smooth-talking serpent shrewdly singled out Eve as the easier target for his silver tongue. As Psalm 55:21 says of false teachers,

> His speech was smoother than butter,
> But his heart was war;
> His words were softer than oil,
> Yet they were drawn swords.

It is a defining feature of false teachers that they appear outwardly as innocent but are inwardly ravening wolves. They do not advertise their nature; they camouflage themselves by flattering their prey: "For such men are slaves, not of our Lord Christ but of their own appetites; and by their smooth and flattering speech they *deceive* the hearts of the *unsuspecting*" (Rom. 16:18; cf. Jude 1:16; emphasis added).

Proverbs 26:28 tells us that while the flatterer finds favor quickly, he later works ruin. By contrast, the one who rebukes a man will initially cause conflict but later find favor (Prov. 28:23).

For churches, feminine social instincts are inversely proportional to ensuring orthodoxy. When women rule, orthodoxy withers. Because of their desire for everyone to play *nice,* they are very likely to approve and endorse flatterers, hirelings, soft men—and equally likely to disapprove and ostracize truth-tellers, shepherds, tough men.

Moreover, when we add loud women into the mix, the problem is multiplied exponentially. They care only for what makes them happy, and flattering false shepherds are eager to enable them. Undue feminine influence thus leads to a spiritual disease well described by Johannes Vos:

The most important element in the purpose of human life is glorifying God, while enjoying God is strictly subordinate to glorifying God. In our religious life, we should always place the chief emphasis on glorifying God. The person who does this will truly enjoy God, both here and hereafter. But the person who thinks of enjoying God apart from glorifying God is in danger of supposing God exists for man instead of man for

God. To stress enjoying God more than glorifying God will result in a falsely mystical and emotional type of religion.[4]

A church in which the influence of women is not checked by masculine rule—where, indeed, it is instead elevated and amplified—will always descend into mystical emotional chaos.

We exist to please God. It is impossible to build true religion on the false assumption of the opposite. Unfortunately, even pious women tend to lead us in that opposite direction if unchecked. And impious, immodest ones only accelerate the move, because they are all about glorifying themselves and their passions rather than glorifying God and His name.

So, why would pastors elevate and amplify women's worst tendencies at the expense of doctrine, discipline, and worship in the first place? It is because women are not the only ones with natural instincts that can be twisted by sin. Men, too, have impulses designed into them that, in their proper place, are good but, removed from it, quickly turn destructive. Two of men's strongest instincts are to elevate women, since they are our glory (1 Cor. 11:7), and to defend them, since they are weaker vessels (1 Pet. 3:7). White knights

4. Johannes Vos, *The Westminster Larger Catechism: A Commentary*, ed. G.I. Williamson (Phillipsburg, NJ: P&R Publishing, 2002), 4.

twist these natural impulses into a mindset that automatically seeks and defers to female approval. They are caught in the grip of a childlike need to validate themselves by defending women. The impulse of valiant deference defines them—and it is enormously destructive, because it makes them easily manipulated weapons for socially able and influential women. These women merely have to take offense at another man, and turn on the waterworks, and the white knights will unreflectively try to destroy him using any means necessary. Moreover, because they are "nice guys," and conditioned in using feminine tactics, they will seldom engage with masculine strategies like direct confrontation and factual refutation. Rather, they will turn to covert maneuvering and character assassination, trying to manipulate the offender into going away through subtle ostracization, turning others against him behind his back.

The overall effect of this white knight/influential women combo is a feedback loop: a vicious circle of social instincts trained toward conforming everyone to agreeable, approved behaviors, rather than to true but often offensive doctrines.

The white knights become chump enforcers for a new orthodoxy based not on the ten commandments but on a new eleventh: *thou shalt be nice and never unmannerly.*

Of course, what is mannerly ultimately comes down to whatever makes the women of both sexes feel good. Wearing yoga pants to church is no violation of the eleventh commandment, because doesn't she have a beautiful figure? But it *is* an egregious violation to point out that she may just as well have painted her legs—because it isn't very nice to make her feel so discomforted, and what kind of pervert notices a woman's beautiful figure anyway?

This feminine-normative mindset is why men's sins are always attacked strongly from the pulpit, but women's sins are barely mentioned. Even the idea of specifically feminine sins does not exist as a category in most pastors' minds. It is why men's ministries are just women's ministries with bacon. It is why a woman can do anything an unordained man can do, and if she gets popular enough to start doing what only ordained men are supposed to do, you had better not notice that she is unordained— or a woman. This is why "whispernets" of nosy biddies routinely undermine faithful ministers who preach the historic position of the Church on sexuality. And it is why we are never surprised to see sizable numbers of other ministers throwing out biblical standards of evidence and conduct in order to support the biddies. A woman is shrieking to be saved from a dragon—what more is there to know?

Thus we find ourselves in the Church Effeminate, where men may either check in their testicles with the usher in skinny jeans, sign a waiver promising not to upset the women, and softly croon about their boyfriend Jesus—or they may be escorted to the door by a mob of valiant heroes who will defend m'lady's honor at any cost.

Thanks to the white knights, men may lay aside their masculinity, or they may lay aside their Christianity. Of course, this is not a real choice; Christianity is innately masculine. But framing is everything—and so if you present men with this dilemma, they will try to choose one of the horns. And since it is a *false* dilemma, whichever way they choose to go, the outworkings are disastrous. They will always end up leaning toward one of two theological errors:

1. MAN AS TRAPPED SPIRIT

If they stick with Christianity, men will typically accept (tacitly or otherwise) that man is a spirit trapped in a prison of flesh. On this view, our human nature is divorced from our biological nature. We are androgynous spirits, and the flesh, far from reflecting our hearts, is an encumbrance to them. This is simply a revival of the ancient Gnostic heresy—a return to pagan spirituality. In his excellent article "Androgyny: The Pagan Sexual Ideal," Dr. Peter Jones explains:

> In the ancient Gnostic texts such connections can be detected. The Church Father Hippolytus, documents how and why the "spiritual" Gnostics did not hesitate to imitate pagan spirituality and sexuality in one form or another. He explains the

Gnostic Naasene participation in the cult of the Goddess. "Because they claimed that everything is spiritual," the Naasenes did not become Galli physically but rather spiritually: "they only perform the functions of those who are castrated" by abstaining from sexual intercourse. So, concludes Hippolytus, the Naasene Gnostics imitate the Galli, the castrated priests of Cybele. "For they urge most severely and carefully that one should abstain, as those men (the Galli) do, from intercourse with women; their behavior otherwise . . . is like that of the castrated." The mythological story of the castration of Attis thus led the Naasenes to conclude that the image of emasculation was a symbol of salvation. Attis cut off his testicles in order to "break with the baser and material world and gain access to immortal life, where there is no longer either male or female." These "Christian" Gnostics sought, through a deep form of spiritual androgyny, a close association with paganism's understanding of salvation.[5]

That this pagan doctrine has been accepted wholesale in the Church is critical to understanding the rampant sexual chaos we are experiencing across all denominations. After all, if there is no *spiritual* distinction between men and women, then it is really just an unfair happenstance that

5. Jones, "Androgyny."

women cannot do the things in the pulpit tradi-tionally reserved to men. They are—in this view—just as qualified psychologically, mentally, and emotionally. If the only reason they are not allowed is because they happen to have female bodies, and God has arbitrarily forbidden people with female bodies from preaching, then surely that is unjust.

This error is thousands of years old. The early Church fought it under the form of Gnosticism, and today we have a neo-Gnosticism. To be a Christian, men are told, you must accept that your male body is toxic.

2. MAN AS BIOLOGICAL MACHINE

The alternative and opposite error, which many men prefer to choose, is that everything about hu-man nature is simply *biological*. This error reduces who we are to our physical appetites and impulses. It takes the standard atheistic, evolutionary view that man is a meat machine, programmed by nat-ural selection to have certain desires. It therefore only follows that there is nothing wrong with em-bracing these natural inclinations.

Whereas the previous error denies the good-ness of the body and defines redemption as the spirit's freedom from it, this error denies the reality of spirit and sees no need for the body's redemp-tion. We are nothing *but* a body, and what we call consciousness is merely an "emergent property" of a complex brain. Moreover, our bodies are not corrupted; they are just a product of evolution, an imperfect process.

Freedom, then, is surrendering to your nature. If it feels good, if it serves your desire, do it.

This error, too, is very old. We see it in Democritus, and also in the schismatic religion of the Sadducees, who "say that there is no resurrection, nor an angel, nor a spirit" (Acts 23:8).

As evidenced by the gender bias in the pews, when men feel forced to choose between these two errors, many prefer the latter. They would rather accept that they are biological machines than that there is something wrong with their bodies. They would rather become materialists and deny the spiritual, than become more feminine to attain spiritual purity. Such "purity" disgusts them—and rightly so. They cannot deny their nature or their desires—such primal, innate forces can't simply be willed away. Masculinity is built into our bodies, and many men would rather lose Christianity than deny their own embodied nature. To do so would be to deny the most foundational reality. It is madness.

Fortunately, neither of the horns of this dilemma is remotely true. We must reject both the pietistic neo-Gnosticism of evangelical androgyny and the mechanistic materialism of evolutionary psychology. Each is paganism. The reality is simple, straightforward biblical anthropology—the doctrine of man.

Biblical anthropology always keeps body and spirit together in a composite. This composite is often called the *soul,* especially in the Hebrew Old Testament. This tradition still lingers in English, as with the saying, "I haven't seen a soul" or the maritime idiom of counting the "souls" aboard a ship.

Human beings are not essentially spirits with bodies merely appended. God did not first create a spirit and then place it into a body. Rather, man was first a body, then God breathed into him the breath of life, and man became a living soul (Gen. 2:7). The body is therefore as truly and eternally a part of man as his spirit. Moreover, the resurrection of that body is central to our salvation. Only in the unity of body and spirit is there a complete person.

Our bodies are gifts from God—good things to be celebrated and honored. Yoda may teach that "luminous beings are we, not this crude matter"—but the Bible doesn't.

By presenting the human person as a soul, as a body and a spirit inseparably bound together, Scripture refutes both errors that modern men are drawn into. Materialism is false because we are a spirit, not just a body. Gnosticism is false because we are a body, not just a spirit. We are neither mere male animals nor androgynous spirits.

Men are men forever. Women are women forever. Binary sexuality is forever. When we die, we will not cease to exist, because we have spirits.

Consciousness is not some emergent property of matter, such that between death and resurrection we experience nothing—for Paul says that to be absent from the body is to be present with the Lord (2 Cor. 5:8). And when we go to be with the Lord in that spirit, we will not become genderless. We will instead, as men without bodies, await the resurrection of those bodies. On the last day, we shall receive glorified and immortal bodies: male bodies that perfectly match and reflect and complete our male spirits—and vice versa. Jerome, one of the early Church fathers, puts it well when he says, "If the woman shall not rise again as a woman nor the man as a man, there will be no resurrection of the body for the body is made up of sex and members."

Salvation is not just a "spiritual" matter that relates only to the spirit, as if the body is largely irrelevant. We are saved in both body and spirit. The spirit is born again; the body will also be redeemed (Rom. 8:23) and transformed to be like our Lord's glorious body (Phil. 3:21). When Paul explains that "you have been bought with a price," he concludes from this argument that you are therefore to "glorify God in [your] body" (1 Cor. 6:20).

This brings us to one last but very important reason that masculine Christian men will submit themselves, at least for a time, to the tyranny of the Church Effeminate. This reason is a bad conscience, derived from improperly ordered masculine drives and desires.

In a word, shame. Shame of things they have done. Shame that they have not honored God with their bodies.

Shame, like pain, is an uncomfortable but necessary teacher. Your conscience is to your spirit as your nerves are to your body. Both move us to turn back from doing something destructive. When you step on a nail, you feel pain—your body is saying, "Stop that." When you sin, you feel shame—your spirit is saying, "Stop that."

Masculinity, because it was created as a powerful force for good, can be twisted by sin into a powerful force for evil. The drive to subdue and rule can be twisted into tyranny, into needless violence, and into a love of money. And that is shameful. Similarly, the drive to be fruitful and multiply can be twisted into fornication, adultery, and every other sexual perversion. That is shameful too. In Philippians 3:19, Paul describes the enemies of Christ: "Their end is destruction; their god is their belly; and they glory in their shame" (ESV). These are men who are slaves to their appetites—and proud of it. Such were some of us (1 Cor. 6:11).

Christian men feel this shame acutely. And it is good that they feel ashamed of twisted masculine desires. It is this shame that drives us all to Christ in repentance. God blesses us with consciences that afflict us when we defile our masculine natures.

The Church Effeminate, for obvious reasons, excels at preaching against and shaming men for their masculine sins. This preaching resonates with men in the throes of repenting of a life dominated by lust and appetite. This can be good—but there is a flip side. This shame can be used against men, to recondition them into thinking that their *masculinity* is the problem, rather than their *sinfulness*. To give an illustration, you should not feel pain when you use your body as designed. When you move an arm or a leg within its normal range of motion, it shouldn't hurt. It should feel just fine. Likewise, you should not feel shame for things that are good and holy. Scripture is clear. It is *good* to be a man. Thus, it is *bad* to feel ashamed of your God-given masculinity.

Our masculine desires are gifts from God. Our duty is not to amputate them—it is to properly harness them.

But due to its neo-Gnosticism and latent misandry, the Church Effeminate will not preach this. Rather, it will try to use men's natural shame at sin as a weapon against them, as the short end of a wedge to separate them from masculinity itself. It will not teach men how the grace of God restores their nature by leading them to repentance, to turning from their sin and toward the glory of masculinity practiced through virtue. Instead, it teaches them to believe that the grace of God eradicates their nature by leading them to effeminacy, to turning from their masculinity and toward a disgusting softness practiced through passivity.

This is justified by arguing that we must focus on the inward spiritual realities.

But while life with Christ is certainly an inward spiritual reality, and it cannot immediately be seen with the eyes, *it does not stay that way.* "Therefore do not let sin reign in your mortal body so that you obey its lusts, and do not go on presenting the members of your body to sin as instruments of unrighteousness; but present yourselves to God as those alive from the dead, and your members as instruments of righteousness to God. For sin shall not be master over you, for you are not under law but under grace" (Rom. 6:12–14).

Paul connects the inward spiritual reality of being dead to sin and alive to Christ with the outer physical reality—what we do with our bodies. Paradoxically, to be freed from the law is to be freed from lawlessness. A slave does what his master tells him to do. Once upon a time, sin was our master, and we served it with our bodies. Inside us were evil desires, and we used our members to accomplish those desires. We lusted with our eyes, we lied with our tongues, and we stole with our hands. Our bodies were instruments of unrighteousness and lawlessness.

But we have been freed from sin. Christ is our Lord now. He is our master.

Being in Christ is like having a seed planted in us. It grows within and slowly expands outside of us through works accomplished in the body. As

James says, "In humility receive the word implanted, which is able to save your souls. But prove yourselves doers of the word, and not merely hearers who delude themselves" (Jas. 1:21–22). As we do this, our tongues preach the truth, sing praises, and taste food unto the glory of God. Our eyes study the creation and learn to love its beauty. Our hands emulate it in our art and architecture, and even our coding. We labor with our backs so that we have enough to provide for ourselves and our families and to give to others.

What once was a tool of evil, now is an instrument of righteousness.

The Church Effeminate has it all backwards. To be a Christian, a man must pick up his masculinity—not lay it down. The real dilemma is not between spirit and body, but between sin's corruption of our sexuality and God's original design. Our sexuality is an essential part of our nature, so much so that a man can be masculine without being virtuous, but he cannot be virtuous without being masculine. The Christian man embraces his sexuality as a good gift from God, and rejects the corruption of this gift by sin.

But the only way to embrace any gift from God is through Jesus Christ. The only way to receive good things from Him is through the power of His gospel. Regaining true manhood is therefore something only possible through the gospel of God's free grace. As Herman Bavinck put it, "Grace serves, not to take up humans into a supernatural order, but to free them from sin. Grace is opposed not to nature, only to sin. . . . Grace restores nature and takes it to its highest pinnacle."[6]

6. Herman Bavinck, *Reformed Dogmatics*, vol. 2, *Sin and Salvation in Christ* (Grand Rapids: Baker, 2006), 577.

8 No Father, No Manhood

NO ONE IS BORN A MAN. NO ONE IS BORN A FATHER.
No one is born a patriarch.

Every boy is born male—but manhood is something into which he must mature. To achieve this, he needs the love and discipline of a father to guide him. In other words, to become a father, you must *have* a father.

Although we may think of fatherhood as a metaphor that we apply to God, Scripture has things the other way around. When Jesus calls God His Father, this is not anthropomorphic language. Rather, when we call men our father, that is theomorphic language. God is the archetypal Father.

This is because to image God, we must first fear him—and our fathers are the ones who teach us this fear. It begins at the earliest age, when we hear the difference between his voice and our mother's: one deeper and stronger, a voice of command; the other softer and nurturing, a voice of comfort. It continues as we begin to learn about his physical presence in our home as the one who compels submission and brings order. We learn that although our mother is bigger than we are, she is the one who feeds us from her own body, who draws us close to warm and comfort us; our father, by contrast, is both bigger still and more distant—a force who brings comfort not by folding us into his body but by *subjecting* us to his body. He has a fearful power to impose order upon us. Indeed, both boys and girls tend to love their father *especially* because he is to be feared. It is precisely because he is dangerous that they value his presence in the family—not because he is dangerous to them but because he is dangerous to the sin and chaos that threatens the harmony of the household. He is the center that holds their world together; if he were not dangerous, he could not defend that world against everything that endangers it and threatens to pull it apart.

Without fathers, sons remain boys. They grow up clueless about how to harness and aim their masculine natures. They are functional bastards.

Clueless bastards are destructive to society because they have not had this fatherhood imaged to them in the way God designed. They are stuck in a state of arrested development, unable to properly image God themselves.

Consider the film *Good Will Hunting*. It follows twenty-year-old janitor Will Hunting, an unrecognized genius. After assaulting a police officer, he is required to see a therapist as part of a deferred prosecution agreement. To legally avoid the therapy, Will uses his genius to find ways to emotionally trigger the therapists assigned to him. One after another they all quit—until he is paired with Sean.

At first, everything seems to go according to plan. Will alienates Sean by insulting his deceased wife in their first session. But Sean is able to see past Will's defense mechanism when he comes to a realization: "You're just a kid. You don't have the faintest idea what you're talking about."

He puts Will in his place with the simple observation that no matter how much he can tell him about Michelangelo, he still has no idea what it smells like in the Sistine Chapel. He has never stood there and looked up at that ceiling. The same is true of women, and war, and love, and loss.

Will is an orphan. He is fatherless. He has tried to compensate for what he should have learned from his father by memorizing entire volumes of books. But his extraordinary ability to do this has only highlighted how ineffective it is at filling the void. Genius or not, he is a paradigm of the clueless bastard. His gifts only magnify the gulf between the knowledge he has and the wisdom he would have inherited from his father.

The power of fathers is undeniable. In *Life Without Father*, Dr. David Popenoe writes, "Involved fathers—especially biological fathers—bring positive benefits to their children that no other person is as likely to bring."[1] Research continues to pile up proving this; 82 percent of father-involvement studies since 1980 have found "significant associations between positive father involvement and off-spring well-being."[2]

Children with strong, active fathers do better. This shows up in surprising ways. For example, there is evidence that a father's overall fitness (not the mother's) is the best indicator of a child's future physical health.[3] We see similar correlation in the areas of educational performance,[4] vocabulary,[5]

---

1. David Popenoe, *Life without Father* (New York: Simon & Schuster, 1996), 163.

2. Paul R. Amato and Fernando Rivera, "Parental Involvement and Children's Behavior Problems," *Journal of Marriage and the Family* 61 (May 1999): 376.

3. R. Figuera Colon, Figueroa-Colon, Reinaldo, et al. "Paternal body fat is a longitudinal predictor of changes in body fat in premenarcheal girls." *The American journal of clinical nutrition* 71.3 (2000): 829–834.

4. "Fathers' and Mothers' Involvement in Their Children's Schools by Family Type and Resident Status," National Center for Education Statistics, Statistical Analysis Report May 2001, https://nces.ed.gov/pubs2001/2001032.pdf

5. Paul Raeburn, *Do Fathers Matter?: What Science Is Telling Us About the Parent We've Overlooked* (New York: Farrar, Strauss, and Giroux, 2015).

and spirituality. Back in 2003, Robbie Low wrote a helpful article in *Touchstone* on the "importance of fathers to churchgoing." In it, he explains,

> In 1994 the Swiss carried out an extra survey that the researchers for our masters in Europe (I write from England) were happy to record. The question was asked to determine whether a person's religion carried through to the next generation, and if so, why, or if not, why not. The result is dynamite. There is one critical factor. It is overwhelming, and it is this: It is the religious practice of the father of the family that, above all, determines the future attendance at or absence from church of the children.[6]

But doesn't the mother play a role? Lowe comments, "In terms of commitment, a mother's role may be to encourage and confirm, but it is not primary to her adult offspring's decision. Mothers' choices have dramatically less effect upon children than their fathers', and without him she has little effect on the primary lifestyle choices her offspring make in their religious observances."[7]

Even long before scientific studies, churchmen knew the straight connection between fathers and the well-being of their households. J.W. Alexander,

6. Robbie Low, "The Truth about Men & Church," *Touchstone* (June 2003).
7. Ibid.

for example, preached: "There is no member of a household whose individual piety is of such importance to all the rest as the father or head. And there is no one whose soul is so directly influenced by the exercise of domestic worship. Where the head of a family is lukewarm or worldly, he will send the chill through the whole house."[8]

The truth of this sinks in when we consider Scripture's own description of households as bodies. The father is the head; the rest of the house is his body. But this means that while a lukewarm father sends a chill through his house, there is nothing so chilling as the cold reality of a home without any father at all. Its icy effects are sobering. In his book *Fatherless Generation*, John Sowers reports,

> According to various sources, children from fatherless homes account for
> - 63 percent of youth suicides
> - 71 percent of pregnant teenagers
> - 90 percent of all homeless and runaway children
> - 70 percent of juveniles in state-operated institutions
> - 85 percent of all youth who exhibit behavior disorders
> - 80 percent of rapists motivated with displaced anger

8. James Waddel Alexander, *Thoughts on Family Worship* (Philadelphia: Presbyterian Board of Publication, 1847), 33.

71 percent of all high school dropouts

75 percent of all adolescents in chemical
abuse centers

85 percent of all youths sitting in prison.[9]

Because the father is the head, as he goes, so goes his household. And as households go, so goes society. The benevolent presence of a father results in a more orderly and fruitful life. His absence, whether by distance or abdication, results in disorder and chaos.

There are all sorts of sociological reasons for the power of fathers, but they boil down to the simple reality that human fathers image God the Father. Just as Jesus, the representation and radiance of God, upholds all things by the word of His power (Heb. 1:3), so human men, the image and glory of God (1 Cor. 11:7), uphold their families, their houses, and their societies by the power entrusted to them, in accordance with the word of God.

The collapse we face today is primarily caused by clueless bastards who don't know how to be fathers—upholders of order. And they don't know this, because they have not had fathers. Or, put another way, they have not been sons.

It is impossible to be a good father without first learning to be a good son. Adam was made to take up the fatherly work of God; this is what

9. John A. Sowers, *Fatherless Generation: Redeeming the Story* (Grand Rapids, MI: Zondervan, 2010), 36–37.

it means to be a son at a fundamental level (e.g., John 5:19–20, 30; 8:28; 14:10). A son represents his father, and thus the most important aspect of his sonship is *becoming* a father. This fatherhood is passed down from generation to generation—from God to Adam to his sons (Gen. 5:3) and all the way to us. It is the natural chain by which God trains up young men to take over the work of their fathers *as* fathers, and to continue His image into the world—establishing order, upholding society, exercising dominion.

A break in the chain of one house can be catastrophic to that house's sons, who find themselves floundering to represent God in the world—not having learned to do this (as an intriguing theological exercise, compare Acts 17:26–27 and Exod. 4:22). But a break in the chain for a whole nation of houses is catastrophic for society itself. A culture that seeks to "smash the patriarchy," that seeks to destroy father-rule, is therefore a culture that seeks its own annihilation. The closer it gets to removing the image of God in father-rule, the closer it gets to unraveling. The further it eliminates the means by which God orders and upholds the human world, the further it descends into chaos. Without the mechanism by which God exercises His dominion over the human world, it can no longer do the work of God: dividing, shaping, filling. It becomes a society of abortion, of butch women, of effeminate men, of gay pride, of belief in gender fluidity, and of every other degrading doctrine that now blurs together that which from the beginning God separated.

"Patriarchy or death" is not a glib catchphrase. It is a seed of vital truth.

Young men today are the unwitting, unwilling beneficiaries of a culture of death. They are clueless bastards in dire need of fathers. They do not know how to image God, and so they do not know how to mature into wise, strong men.

So it's too late, right? Your father failed you in whatever way, and now you're stuck being Will Hunting, perpetually trying to learn from books or blogs or YouTube?

No. God has provided fathers.

Unfortunately, many clueless bastards are looking in the wrong place. They are trying to fill the father void by turning to *teachers*—who promise *knowledge*—rather than to *fathers* who will disciple them into *wisdom*. They want easily obtained learning, rather than hard-won and practical wisdom. They are eager to exercise authority, without themselves being placed under authority. They are like Simon the Magician, seeking to gain the power of God through money, when they should be like the Hebrews, seeking to gain the holiness of God through chastening: "If ye endure chastening, God dealeth with you as with sons; for what son is he whom the father chasteneth not? But if ye be without chastisement, whereof all

are partakers, then are ye bastards, and not sons"
(Heb. 12:7–8, KJV).

By turning to guides, rather than to fathers, they
are doing what comes naturally—unwittingly seeking to remain bastards. They don't see the value in
becoming sons, because in their case they cannot
relate to the verses that follow: "Furthermore, we
had earthly fathers to discipline us, and we respect-
ed them; shall we not much rather be subject to the
Father of spirits, and live? For they disciplined us
for a short time as seemed best to them, but He disciplines us for our good, so that we may share His
holiness" (Heb. 12:9–10).

But Paul, in writing to the clueless Corinthians,
exhorts them, "I do not write these things to make
you ashamed, but to admonish you as my beloved
children. For though you have countless *guides* in
Christ, you do not have many *fathers.* For I became
your father in Christ Jesus through the gospel. I
urge you, then, be imitators of me" (1 Cor. 4:14–16,
ESV; emphasis added).

Sonship is *imitative.* It is not something learned
from afar, but something learned by participating in another man's life. So it cannot be picked
up from YouTube or from blogs or from books—it
must be absorbed through actively partaking in the
life of the man whose son you wish to be. At the risk
of stating the obvious, that participation is as his
son; not as his peer or his bro. It means being under
his authority, under his discipline. In other words,

sonship involves *real life discipling*, as Paul immediately goes on to show:

> That is why I sent you Timothy, my beloved and
> faithful child in the Lord, to remind you of my
> ways in Christ, as I teach them everywhere in ev-
> ery church. Some are arrogant, as though I were
> not coming to you. But I will come to you soon,
> if the Lord wills, and I will find out not the talk
> of these arrogant people but their power. For the
> kingdom of God does not consist in talk but in
> power. What do you wish? Shall I come to you
> with a rod, or with love in a spirit of gentleness?
> (1 Cor. 4:17–21, ESV)

Not having been built up from childhood, clueless bastards are often too fragile to easily cope
with being sons. They are created for sonship, and
so they *long* for fathers—which is why they idolize men they can look up to as leaders. But being
damaged from childhood, they do it from a distance—disembodied. They learned young that
they must order their own worlds, that *they* must
defend themselves from threats, that *they* must
be the strong ones in their own lives. But a child
cannot teach himself these things, and so clueless
bastards tend to be undisciplined, defensive, and
brittle. They find it hard to endure the chastening
that produces the fruit of righteousness, avoiding
it when they can and chafing against it when they

cannot. They seek new ways of being sons that aren't so hands-on, ways that mimic the neo-Gnostic tendencies of our age. Sons in spirit, through the internet, but not in body, through participation in another man's life.

This doesn't work. God created us as embodied creatures, where the physical and the spiritual are intertwined. This means that the physical *matters*. Clueless bastards frequently don't understand this, or outright reject it, because they have not experienced it. They think they can replace what God has made with an abstract facsimile, recreating the intimacy of fraternity in the form of text on a screen.

But we are not living in the Matrix. Embodied existence is the only way for human males to truly participate in the experience of other men. Our design matters. "Though I have much to write to you, I would rather not use paper and ink. Instead I hope to come to you and talk face to face, so that our joy may be complete" (2 John 12; cf. 3 John 1:13, ESV).

Fathers love sons. Love requires physical connection. The internet can both supplement and facilitate this love—but it can never replace it. Paul describes love as the perfect bond of unity (Col. 3:14). Its origin is God Himself, who *is* love—three persons participating in each other with such unity that they are one being. This unity, this "onetogetherness," is something men are made for—but online fellowship is merely a shadow of it. You can no more have digital onetogetherness than you can have digital sex. You can't cheat God's natural order.

Where are you to find fathers in real life, then? If your own father has failed you, where can you go? Well, sonship and fatherhood start in the natural household—but that is by no means the full extent of what God made us for. In God's own household, there are no orphans. There are no bastards. There are *only* sons. The gospel is a gospel of sonship:

> For all who are led by the Spirit of God are sons of God. For you did not receive the spirit of slavery to fall back into fear, but you have received the Spirit of adoption as sons, by whom we cry, "Abba! Father!" The Spirit himself bears witness with our spirit that we are children of God, and if children, then heirs—heirs of God and fellow heirs with Christ, provided we suffer with him in order that we may also be glorified with him . . . And we know that for those who love God all things work together for good, for those who are called according to his purpose. For those whom he foreknew he also predestined to be conformed to the image of his Son, in order that he might be the firstborn among many brothers. And those whom he predestined he also called, and those whom he called he also justified, and those whom he justified he also glorified. (Rom. 8:14–17, 28–30, ESV)

Sonship is the antidote to clueless bastardry, and God is the great, archetypal Father—even to those who are fatherless (Ps. 68:5). We don't say that believing the gospel will fix all the childhood damage of fatherlessness, or transform you into a mature man. Believing the gospel is the necessary *first step* to fixing the childhood damage of father-lessness, and doing so will eventually *bring about* your transformation into a mature man, through the household of God. Scripture establishes a social order through which God's fatherhood is represented by men, to sons in the faith.

"I write so that you will know how one ought to conduct himself in the household of God, which is the church of the living God, the pillar and support of the truth" (1 Tim. 3:15). The Church is the house-hold of God, and so there is a right way to conduct yourself within her. Just as in the natural family you are to honor your father and submit yourself to his discipline, so in the spiritual family. Here, pastors are the spiritual fathers. As we saw in 1 Corinthians 4, Paul was a father to the Corinthians—not by apostleship but *through the gospel* (v. 15). The Corinthians were failing to grow up to be mature sons of God because they had too many guides and too few fathers. Pastors are a central means by which God brings His children into maturity:

And He gave some as apostles, and some as proph-ets, and some as evangelists, *and some as pas-*

tors and teachers, for the equipping of the saints for the work of service, to the building up of the body of Christ; until we all attain to the unity of the faith, and of the knowledge of the Son of God, *to a mature man,* to the measure of the stature which belongs to the fullness of Christ. As a result, we are no longer to be children, tossed here and there by waves and carried about by every wind of doctrine, by the trickery of men, by craftiness in deceitful scheming; but speaking the truth in love, we are to *grow up* in all aspects into Him who is the head, even Christ, from whom the whole body, being fitted and held together by what every joint supplies, according to the proper working of each individual part, causes the growth of the body for the building up of itself in love. (Eph. 4:11–16; emphasis added)

Do you want to be a mature man? The sort of man who isn't tossed to and fro like a clueless bastard? This requires a pastor, a spiritual father who will shepherd and discipline you, to help you to grow in holy wisdom. It is God's design. That is how He orders His house.

Do you think you are a mature man, but you consider a pastor unnecessary in your life? God is not mocked. What a man sows, so shall he reap; a child who spurns the correction of his father grows to be a fool. You cannot represent God's rule without submitting to Him as Father—and you cannot submit to Him as Father without submitting to His design for His household. This is as true for would-be patriarchs who stiffen their necks against God's hierarchy as it is for feminists who do the same.

Now, it is true that many pastors are *not* good fathers. But it is equally true that most clueless bastards are nitpicky sons. God says you need a pastor—not a hero. It can be easy to idolize a man from afar, especially online; but real-world relationships reveal a man's imperfections, failings, and sins. The idealist will resent a pastor who is a real man. He desires a hero to emulate, a man who never disappoints. But no such man exists in the real world, with the exception of the God-Man.

And yet Christ commands us to submit ourselves to imperfect men.

A father should not be a clone of yourself. Neither must he conform to your own pet expectations in order to disciple you well. God has set the qualifications (Tit. 1:6–9; 1 Tim. 3:1–7; cf. 4:6–16). If you're submitting yourself to His fatherhood, you will accept those qualifications—even if you think you could improve on them. *Especially* if you think you could improve on them.

This doesn't mean you should settle for anything. The qualifications do have to be met. A majority of churches fail at this, and so they will not disciple you well. A majority of pastors are themselves clueless bastards, weak in constitution and effeminate in conduct—nothing like the

tough shepherds of old, who in more modern parlance we might call cowboys. Trying to submit to
them is an exercise in futility and frustration, and
ultimately will score the lines of resentment and
immaturity even deeper into a clueless bastard's
psyche. But the West is still Christian *enough* that
anyone *can* be near a church with good fathers—if
it really matters to him.

In *Life Together*, Bonhoeffer writes, "Those who
love their dream of a Christian community more
than the Christian community itself become de-
stroyers of that Christian community, even though
their personal intentions may be ever so honest,
earnest, and sacrificial."[10]

These are men that Bonhoeffer calls visionary
dreamers. They are never satisfied with anything
in the real world because it doesn't live up to their
ideal. Many men today are such visionary dreamers. They are on a quest to find a church that only
exists in their imaginations. It is a church that
lives up to every expectation for their perfect litur-
gy, their perfect preaching, their perfect doctrine,
their perfect music—and their perfect pastor. It is
led by a hero they can look up to. It is filled with
people that are "likeminded" in the dreamer's
niche concerns. That church is out there. He just
knows it is. He hasn't found it yet—so far, every

10. Dietrich Bonhoeffer, *Life Together: The Classic Exploration
of Christian Community*, trans. John W. Doberstein (New York:
Harper & Row, 1927), 27.

church has been off in some way. So he will hop from one church to the next, always looking for something better. He is vocal about the terrible condition of the modern local church, and often gives up entirely on it, turning exclusively to the internet. Thank goodness for podcasts and social media. How else could he get his "preaching" and "fellowship"?

We are walking a tightrope between the compromise of gutless pastors and the delusions of visionary dreamers.

There is no perfect church.

However, there are faithful churches. Find one. If you are genuinely in a region where the only church options are terrible, you have three potential courses of action:

1. Work for reformation where you are;
2. Move to a region where there is a good church;
3. Join an effort to plant a new church in your region.

That's it. Sitting at home isn't an option. Complaining isn't an option. Pick one and get to work.

God's house-rules are not optional. God's design for embodied creation is not optional. Hence church is not optional. The internet can guide you, but it will not father you. The only way to become a mature son of God, to become a true father yourself, is through the means He established by which He raises up sons to image Him.

The formula is simple: Find a church that will disciple you. Submit yourself to it. Grow up.

9 No Gravitas, No Manhood

FOR A MAN, THE SAYING "GROW UP" MIGHT BE better translated "Get gravitas."

Gravitas is not a term you hear much today, but it is one of vital importance to recovering masculine piety—that is, masculine duties to God and man. Without gravitas, we cannot reestablish an order in our culture that reflects God's word.

Gravitas was a Roman virtue, referring to a man's seriousness, his dignity, his *weight*. It is a useful term because Scripture also speaks of weight in a similar way. The Hebrew word *kabod* is usually translated *glory* or *honor* when speaking of persons, but the word literally means "to weigh heavily." In

Psalm 19:1, for instance, the heavens are telling of the *kabod* of God—His greatness, His honor, His weightiness. In Genesis 12:10, the famine was *kabod* in the land. In Genesis 13:2, Abram is very *kabod* in cattle and silver and gold—he is weighty with weighty things. And in Genesis 34:19, Shechem was *kabod* above all the house of his father.

A man of *kabod* is a man of substance. A man who leaves an impression, like a rock leaves an impression in the earth. The necessity of this is imaged even in our very bodies: men are heavier and taller and hairier than women; their voices are deeper; their muscles are stronger. These simple facts *mean things.*

While *kabod* and gravitas are intimately related ideas, they are not exactly the same. The difference between them is that *kabod* can be bestowed; gravitas must be recognized. In other words, one can be had without earning it; the other *must* be earned. For instance, the young son of a king has *kabod* simply because he is royalty. Whether or not he is good, or strong, or wise, or courageous, or skillful, his station is one that demands greater honor. He has *kabod* by lot. He *can* earn *more,* but he already has more of it than most—and he didn't earn what he was born to. Christian men are in a similar situation: we have *kabod* because we participate in the glory of the Lord Jesus. Having been covenantally incorporated into Him through the Spirit, we share in everything He has (cf. Heb. 3:14;

12:10). This is unmerited—a gift that we do not in any way deserve.

By contrast, gravitas is not something we can be born with, nor reborn into. It is not so much *bestowed* as it is *recognized*—which means that it must first be earned. Although sometimes charisma can be mistaken for gravitas, and charismatic men can fake it for a while, this is only a cheap imitation—a hollow facsimile that will collapse under pressure. Despite your best efforts, you cannot actually *be* more weighty than you are. The scribes and Pharisees liked to stand on the street corners and sound trumpets and wear large phylacteries and long tassels to look important—but that didn't give them gravitas. People instantly saw the difference between them, and the much younger Jesus: "They were amazed at His teaching; for He was teaching them as one having authority, and not as the scribes" (Mark 1:22).

Here is another way to think of this: *kabod* is the image of God—glory and honor is *inherent* in it. It is granted by deed—originally to Adam, who ruined it, and then to Jesus, who restored the "radiance of His glory and the exact representation of His nature" (Heb. 1:3). When we become benefactors of this deed, of the New Covenant, we too are granted *kabod*. But gravitas is the *fruit* of imaging God. It is *kabod* on legs.

Gravitas is the result of having settled into your Christian identity as a man. It is what happens when you become proficient at reflecting the glory you were made to reflect. You *are* the image and glory of God (1 Cor. 11:7); you *get* gravitas by habitually *living* as such, abiding in Jesus (John 15:5), and conforming yourself ever more closely to His infinitely weighty image. Gravitas is, essentially, an effect of developing virtue, which finds its source in God, and thus conforms you to His image. This virtue is gained by practicing the duties that God has given you, and these duties are tied up in working toward the mission that He created you for. We will be so bold as to say that an unbeliever can only ever develop gravitas inasmuch as he emulates the kind of virtue that comes from devotion to the mission of God. This is because he cannot properly image God any other way, and gravitas is the fruit of imaging God. Whatever gravitas a man has is a dim reflection of the infinite weight of Yahweh.

Men in hell have no gravitas.

To gain gravitas, you must become more like Jesus. You must develop virtue. This requires spiritual fathers, which is why Paul tells Titus to instruct the older men to be "grave." He does not mean something like "deathly serious," but rather, in the words of Calvin, there should be "a becoming gravity" in the lives of elder men, which should compel the young to modesty. The spiritual weight of these men should be such that their "gravitational pull" draws younger men into a nearer orbit with God. Gravity itself is a useful analogy. It pulls things into their proper place. It brings and maintains order. If it were to cease, we would all start floating helplessly. Our solar system would be reduced to chaotic chunks of rock spinning wildly into the void. So it is with gravitas. It establishes order and regularity; without it, our cosmos falls into disorder and chaos.

Because gravitas comes from God, the only way to start getting it is by making a practice of meditating on the gravitas of God. You must know it before you can start considering how you wish to reflect it. You must be a man of the Word before you can be thoroughly equipped for training in righteousness (2 Tim. 3:17). Only by knowing the character of God, and His will for man, will you be able to accurately pursue the duties, and develop the virtues, that will produce gravitas.

You must be a man who knows God well enough to fear Him.

The fear of God is something almost unheard of in modern Christianity—yet Scripture is perfectly plain: you cannot image God if you do not fear Him. Consider how Proverbs, written to a young man, opens with a statement of its purpose—that its reader should gain wisdom—and concludes this with a warning: "The fear of the LORD is the beginning of knowledge; fools despise wisdom and instruction" (Prov. 1:7).

What should we infer from this? The Bible often tailors its warnings to our sinful tendencies; it does not warn men against nagging, nor women against being doormats. Rather, it warns husbands against their tendency to despise and neglect their wives; wives against disrespecting and controlling their husbands. It is therefore safe to conclude from Proverbs 1:7 that young men tend to have trouble fearing God. They are cocky, arrogant—and this false bravado is a sin they must overcome to be truly wise.

Proverbs mentions the fear of the Lord fourteen times, triangulating on a set of attributes and behaviors that you can look for in yourself, and in others. We won't itemize each one, but it is helpful to consider the highlights:

1. **A man who fears the Lord gives and receives instruction and rebuke, so as to become more like his Father.** By contrast, a man who does not fear God hates and scoffs at anything that requires him to admit error or change his ways. This fragile vanity means he can never be intimately acquainted with God or His ways. He hasn't the patience or inclination to diligently search out what is right and true; he wants only to indulge and vindicate himself.

2. **A man who fears the Lord hates evil—especially pride, arrogance, and perverted speech.** These grieve him, and he tries to avoid them. By contrast, a man who does not fear God is himself evil—he is boastful and

NO GRAVITAS, NO MANHOOD

disrespectful, hasty to judge others, and eager to involve himself in speaking ill of them.

3. **A man who fears the Lord is content to be made low because he understands how he compares to God.** This man seeks his true place before Him, and so he naturally raises up God's greatness rather than his own. By contrast, a man who does not fear God seeks to establish superiority over everyone, including God.

4. **A man who fears the Lord trusts the Lord.** Because his refuge is God, he is firm even in crisis or poverty, and his children can take refuge in him. He is a true patriarch, because he is a son of the True Patriarch. But a man who does not fear God is fearful of what people will do, even when circumstances seem very favorable. He frets for the future.

The central theme of Proverbs is Solomon teaching his son the trade of wise rulership. At a higher level, it is also God teaching us the same thing: the trade of dominion, of how to be His sons by faithfully representing Him. A son is one who reveals and represents his father, as Jesus taught us (John 5:19–20). This is our calling. Deuteronomy 10:12–13 helps us understand how the fear of God ties into this calling of sonship, describing what God requires of us, namely, "to fear the LORD your God, to walk in all His ways and love Him, and to serve the LORD your God with all your heart and with all your soul, and to keep the LORD's commandments and His statutes. . . ."

To fear God is to love Him and to walk in His ways. It is to accurately represent Him and rule for Him. It is to worship Him by serving Him in every part of your life. It is to be a true son as Adam was created to be, and as Jesus was. But sin twists the desire to rule in God's name into a craving to rule in our own. And it starts young. This is why Solomon warns his son to fear God. A young man must first choose to fear God before he can ever hope to be *like* God—to be *weighty*. If you would be feared, you must learn fear. You must turn from your own wisdom and strength to find true wisdom and strength in God. You must put self-rule to death in order to truly rule.

Sin is slippery. We justify rebellious tendencies in ourselves, and we want to think the best of others. Yet the Bible says to examine the fruit. While there are, of course, all manner of fruit you could examine, Jesus and James point us to one that is especially important to accurately assess which direction you are moving in your fear of the Lord. This is your speech toward God, and toward his delegates. Out of the heart, the mouth speaks.

While there are myriad ways in which our speech betrays us, there is one example that makes the point especially cuttingly: our use of simple colloquialisms like "holy cow" and "holy crap."

These are a terribly common way that we betray our lack of fear for God. Saying them is so instinctive that we don't think about it at all. But what do the seraphs continually sing before the heavenly throne? "Holy, Holy, Holy, is the LORD of hosts, the whole earth is full of His glory" (Isa. 6:3). This holiness is the devastating divinity of God. Isaiah is undone by this fearsome otherness.

In Exodus 20:7, God instructs us not to take up His name for a worthless cause. As observed in the NET Bible translation notes, "The command prohibits use of the name for any idle, frivolous, or insincere purpose. . . . The name is to be treated with reverence and respect because it is the name of the holy God."[1]

So what do we say about the holy God when we take this one attribute—His holiness—that defines Him above all else . . . and use it as an adjective to describe excrement in a banal expression of mild surprise? Can there be any more vain, frivolous, or insincere purpose?

Jesus says we will give an account for every worthless or idle word we utter. No doubt there will be many, many of these for each of us. But a powerful way to gain gravitas is to gain increasing mastery of your tongue. A good first step down this path is to determine not to irreverence and disrespect the very nature of God from which gravitas

1. Exodus 20, note 21, NET Bible, accessed August 26, 2021, https://netbible.org/bible/Exodus+20.

stems. After that, you can work on other minced blasphemies like "Oh my gosh," which simply emulate the form and sound of something you know is wrong to say—while pretending that this isn't what you're doing because you swapped out a letter or two.

Our speech about God is one good check. But since all fatherhood is from God, how a young man speaks to older men is another basic acid test of how he regards God Himself. Leviticus 19:32 makes the connection explicit: "You shall rise up before the grayheaded and honor the aged, and you shall revere your God." This is a simple application of the fifth commandment. As the Westminster Larger Catechism observes, "By father and mother, in the fifth commandment, are meant, not only natural parents, but all superiors in age and gifts; and especially such as, by God's ordinance, are over us in place of authority, whether in family, church, or commonwealth."[2]

We have argued at length that the modern world hates hierarchy. Many of the men we speak to are highly receptive to hearing this—as long as we only speak of how wicked and Satanic it is to blur the hierarchy between man and woman. They are much less eager to hear the same thing about flattening the hierarchies between old and young. But the principle is identical, and so the question

2. Question 124.

is simple: Do you flatten out age-status in order to treat your elders as equals? Do you speak to them like they're your buddies or your bros? Or are you even a straight-up punk, treating them as inferiors? Do you presume to mock them or rebuke them (cf. 2 Kgs. 2:23–24), or do you show them honor?

Even Timothy, directly commissioned by the apostle Paul to straighten out the false teaching in Ephesus, was told, "Do not sharply rebuke an older man, but rather appeal to him as a father" (1 Tim. 5:1). God represents His fatherhood through the created order, and how a younger man speaks to the older men in his life reflects how he treats God in his heart. It tells you what he *really* thinks of gravitas— and whether he is serious about gaining it.

But this leads us to a common pitfall. Remember that to be grave is not to be deathly serious. There is a tension here that you must navigate, a path between two ditches. To have gravitas means to be taken seriously as a man; unfortunately, many men who desire gravitas therefore become puffed up with their own perceived importance. They take themselves very seriously—yet no one else does. It is not hard to spot a self-serious man like this. You will usually notice that he cannot laugh at anything, least of all himself. He fears levity, because in making light of something, he might himself be thought light. He appears to have a solemn manner—but it is really the grimace of bearing a crushing burden. He is an overloaded bridge creaking under too much weight, and this fragility comes from lacking discernment. It is true that you should not be self-abasing or always retreating into irony. You should not make yourself the butt of your own jokes. But you must nonetheless have the basic ability to distinguish between what is actually weighty and what is not. There are many things, for instance, that you *should* make light of.

> The kings of the earth take their stand
> And the rulers take counsel together
> Against the LORD and against His Anointed, saying,
> "Let us tear their fetters apart
> And cast away their cords from us!"
> He who sits in the heavens laughs,
> The Lord scoffs at them. (Ps. 2:2–4)

The self-serious man is unable to distinguish truly weighty matters and circumstances from those deserving of laughter and scoffing. The reason for this is typically that his most fundamental point of error is in assessing his *own* weight. He cannot separate making light of something from being perceived as a lightweight, so he fears to laugh at all. By taking himself too seriously (Rom. 12:3), he signals that he is unreliable and untrustworthy—and, ironically, this ensures that others cannot take him seriously. If you have ever met someone who is afraid to laugh or mock for fear of what others will think—"damaging the witness" in Christian parlance—you have probably met a self-serious man who is trying to fake gravitas.

On the other hand, levity can also lead into a ditch. We must be grave about the weighty things and enjoy levity with the light ones. But levity can be a relief for men who are trying to figure out gravitas. It is an escape from the burden of a weight that they have not yet developed the spiritual muscles to lift. Many men are thus inadvertently drawn from levity into flippancy. C.S. Lewis saw the same problem in his generation:

> [Humor] is invaluable as a means of destroying shame. If a man simply lets others pay for him, he is "mean"; if he boasts of it in a jocular manner and twits his fellows with having been scored off, he is no longer "mean" but a comical fellow. . . . Cruelty is shameful—unless the cruel man can represent it as a practical joke. A thousand bawdy, or even blasphemous, jokes do not help towards a man's damnation so much as his discovery that almost anything he wants to do can be done, not only without the disapproval but with the admiration of his fellows, if only it can get itself treated as a joke.[3]

Do you see the connection? Calvin stated that a lack of gravity would encourage immodesty and

3. C.S. Lewis, *The Screwtape Letters* (1942; New York: HarperOne, 2009), 55.

youthful wantonness—what the 1828 Webster's describes as "sportiveness and negligence of restraint." It is the same thing that Screwtape wants to see cultivated in Wormwood's "patient." He wants unrestrained sin to be excused as "just playing." Everything becomes part of a game. There is no shame. Nothing is serious.

Since Lewis's time, we have become a culture awash in immodesty and youthful wantonness—we are a cult of youth. "OK, boomer," we tell our elders. We are also a culture awash in frivolous entertainment—and especially comedy, which has a special place in the heart of our culture. It has a special appeal to our guilty souls because flippancy can be used as a kind of atonement ritual. The comedian is our modern priest, standing on a high place before us, publicly confessing our terrible deeds, our guilty habits, our wicked thoughts—and removing the shame by turning it all into a joke.

Funny enough, comedians tend to be depressed. There was only ever one man who could truly take on the sins of the world—and even He had to die to do it. Looking into the abyss of a darkened heart takes a toll. "My dad's humor came from life, and I don't think Dad had a choice," Richard Pryor's daughter Rain said in *I Am Richard Pryor*, a documentary on the comedian's life. "You either laugh your way through it, or you die through it."

We emphasize both ditches here because, just as two sides of a coin have more in common than the twelfth of an inch that separates them, there is not actually much difference between the joker and the self-serious man. Both are trying to deal with reality in their own power, and both lack the strength to do so. The joker, in his fear, makes everything light so he does not feel the weight; he is never serious, so no one takes him seriously. The self-serious man, in his pride, makes everything heavy; his artificial weight is obvious, so no one takes him seriously either. But we *should* find funny things funny, and we *should* take serious things seriously. Only in a man who has the wisdom to rightly discern which is which and the strength to obey reality—often against peer pressure—can gravitas be born and nurtured. And this returns us to the beginning: to meditating on the character of God and being well-instructed in His ways.

Calvin says that gravitas is "procured by well-regulated morals."[4] To discern between good and evil, between wisdom and foolishness, is to have the foundation of gravitas. The grave man is a man who has learned wisdom. He has trained himself in rightly judging and ordering both himself and his world. His very presence exerts force that orders those around him. He is a bulwark against chaos.

But the inverse is equally true. A society lacking in grave men is a society abundant in social *dis*order. Men without gravity are, consciously or not,

---

4. John Calvin, commentary on Titus 2:2.

agents of chaos. Calvin observes, "Nothing is more shameful than for an old man to indulge in youthful wantonness, and, by his countenance, to strengthen the impudence of the young."[5] If this statement brings the image of certain pastors and magistrates and celebrities unbidden into your mind, you are not alone. We are a culture awash in wantonness and impudence. A dearth of grave men has had a destabilizing influence. How shall we reverse it?

5. John Calvin, commentary on Titus 2:2.

10 Gravitas through Duty

IT IS BY GRACE THAT WE ARE ABLE TO GAIN gravitas. By grace we have our orbits corrected as God becomes the center of our universe. By grace we procure the well-regulated morals of which Calvin speaks. By grace we are "being transformed into the same image from glory to glory, just as from the Lord, the Spirit" (2 Cor. 3:18). This is how God adds His own glory, His own weight, to our lives.

But He does not merely do this *to* us; He does it *with* us. Grace is God's undeserved *help* in doing what He made us to do from the beginning: to carry His rule into creation. Our job is to continue the task that He began in the creation week, rightly ordering the world, forming and filling it.

God has given us masculine desires to get us to accomplish this task. Our powerful drives, properly directed, are a great blessing, propelling us along the path to glory. They are what compel us to exercise dominion—over ourselves and our world. Dominion is our duty. It is how we image God, how we are transformed from glory to glory, how we gain gravitas. We already *have* it as a gift, which is why it can be transformed from glory to glory. And because we have it, we must *exercise* it, to increase in excellence. We don't earn the right to dominion. It is already built into our nature as men. What we do need to earn is the *ability* to use this gift well. Proper dominion—true imaging of God—begins with your willing acceptance to do this. It means intentionally taking up the right and responsibility to *represent God.* In other words, you must be committed to establishing right order in your world, as God would have you do, and according to no other standard. This is right masculinity, modeled after the perfect man, our Lord Jesus.

But if dominion is a responsibility, a duty, then we should expect there to be rules to follow. And there are indeed certain key requirements that are foundational to our masculinity—duties that tell us more or less what exercising our dominion looks like. These are, in turn, related to virtues, because what we ought to *do* reflects how we ought to *be.*

Let's start with these virtues, as it will help us to better understand the duties.

There is a triad of masculine virtues that we can derive directly from Scripture. These are unique ways in which men are to be holy. They are mutually dependent, mutually reinforcing areas where, if you fail, you fail not just as a *Christian* but as a *man*.

The first is **wisdom.** This is your grasp of what is happening in your world, and how to act accordingly. Right judgment for the purpose of right order. Wisdom is informed first by your fear and knowledge of the Lord and His word, and second by your understanding of your world at large. When we said that getting gravitas starts by meditating upon God's word, we were really saying that getting gravitas starts by steeping yourself in God's own wisdom. You practice developing this virtue by conforming your mind to God's. It is both the first step and the final destination.

Though both men and women ought to seek wisdom, women are instructed to seek it from men: from their husbands (1 Cor. 14:35; cf. Eph. 5:26) and from their pastors—who are in turn selected out of the men in the Church for their special skill at their husbandly duties (1 Tim. 3:1–7). This makes being wise an especially masculine obligation. A man is required by God to wisely order his world, including those over whom he is the head. How can a man teach his wife and children if he does not first have wisdom himself? Even the analogy of head and body has wisdom bound up in it; the man is, put crudely, the brains of the operation. A husband who lacks wisdom, therefore, is failing in his duties as a man. Fortunately, he can in turn ask God, who gives wisdom generously and without reproach to all who come to him in faith (Jas. 1:5–8).

The second virtue is **workmanship.** This is your developed ability in the talents God has given you; the skills you need in order to exercise dominion. It is, in a sense, wisdom put into action. We use the word *workmanship* because most of your success does not depend on *skill* or *mastery* necessarily— nor even, to begin with, on *competence.* We know many men with great skill and talent, who nonetheless achieve little because they will not work. And we know many other men who have achieved great mastery, but over worthless things. What God wants, more than genius, is simple willingness to work hard where He has placed you. Remember that He has made you to serve—this is your spiritual worship. The term *workmanship* thus emphasizes the ongoing nature of service: of perfecting your craft through labor. Obviously, competence, skill, and mastery are all great things. God wants you to make glorious use of your gifts. But to achieve such excellence requires, fundamentally, faithful workmanship.

Again, women can be known for workmanship, and they should seek to develop it. They worship through service also. But workmanship is about more than simply *doing;* it is about becoming *useful.* This is a uniquely masculine quality. To see this, simply consider the difference between what women look for in a man and what men look for in a woman. At a simplistic level, women see men as *success* objects; men see women as *sex* objects. Men look for external and internal beauty; women look for active and potential utility. Our desires for the opposite sex reflect the baseline purpose of that sex, the foundational design, the way in which they fulfill their duties of dominion—and utility is what workmanship is all about. This is why it is integral to masculinity in a way that it is not to femininity.

The third virtue is **strength.** It is, of course, intimately connected to workmanship, just as workmanship is to wisdom—yet it is also a virtue in its own right. Indeed, strength is the most stereotypically masculine virtue. It is exemplified in the exaggerated sexual dimorphism of mankind—we are 60–100 percent stronger than women.

Although strength is multifaceted, perhaps the most helpful way to think of it is the ability to do work while bearing weight. This, of course, ties it back to gravitas, to weightiness and glory. The body is made to reflect the soul, and so Scripture often places strength of body alongside strength of mind in the proverbial phrase "be strong and courageous." Strength is the fortitude through which you stand firm under pressure, through which you translate the virtue of wisdom into action. It is the firmness of asserting rather than retiring, the hardness of conquering rather than surrendering, the force by which we do and dare. Strength penetrates and divides, overcomes and shapes, prevails and subdues. A woman who is strong like this is butch and unnatural; a man who is *not* is gay—and equally unnatural.

Strength as a defining virtue of masculinity is sadly obscured in many modern Bibles; for instance, in 1 Kings 2:2 the Hebrew literally reads "be strong and as a man," and in Isaiah 46:8 it reads "show yourselves men." By the same token, 1 Cor. 16:13 brings together the virtue of strength and the duty of guarding, which we will discuss shortly, saying, "Be on the alert, stand firm in the faith, act like men, be strong." For a woman to be weak is no shame to her; she is made as the weaker vessel (1 Pet. 3:7). For a man to be weak is worthy of scorn:

> The mighty men of Babylon have ceased fighting,
> They stay in the strongholds;
> Their strength is exhausted,
> They are becoming like women. (Jer. 51:30; cf.
>   Isa. 19:16)

Strength is a special problem for modern men. Workmanship is sometimes neglected, especially in

young men tempted into escaping into fake dominion through playing video games or binge-watch-
ing shows. But most men must still work to eat. And
wisdom is often elevated even to the level of an idol.
We can cultivate it in abundance if we are motivated; our access to knowledge is unparalleled, and
the "knowledge economy" has given this a certain
glamour in the modern day. Moreover, the Church
has for centuries emphasized wisdom, to the point
that it has fallen captive to the cult of Athens, always seeking respectability in the academic world
and fearing to be cool-shamed for thinking God's
"backwards" thoughts.

Whenever there is an unbalanced emphasis on
one virtue, it can become a vice. This happens simply because each virtue must be *applied* in another.
Wisdom without the strength to put it into action is
worthless. Strength without wise application is destructive. Workmanship without wisdom is toil and
futility, and so on.

If you are reading this, you probably have a good
idea how to cultivate wisdom, and most likely an
inkling of how to go about improving your workmanship. But how do you cultivate strength—especially since, if you're the average, your *work* no
longer requires manual labor?

This book is not an instruction manual for
getting swole. There are plenty of those already.
(Bnonn likes *Easy Strength*. Michael prefers a simple Olympic lifting routine.) What you use doesn't

matter; just get strong. This is not optional; a weak man is no man at all, and you will not understand what we mean by this unless and until you actually are strong. But physical strength is not the only kind you need. Without mental fortitude, the strongest muscles are of no value whatsoever. The kingdom of God is not a matter of food and drink or macros and reps, but of righteousness. In that vein, here are five things that nearly every modern man should stop doing immediately to become less weak, gain spiritual strength, and get gravitas:

1. **Stop seeking praise.** This is the base motivation of virtue-posturing social justice warriors and thirsty white knights. They perform their good works to be noticed. Why? In John 12, Jesus says "they loved the approval of men rather than the approval of God" (v. 43). Seeking the praise of men, and especially of women, demonstrates weakness in a man: you are compliant to the perceptions of others, rather than commanding your own world, and having it in turn commanded by God. The Lord knows the quality of your work. He sees all. Live for his praise (Col. 3:22). The confident man knows where he has failed and has spoken with God about it. You should not be ashamed of enjoying praise—men naturally respond to being honored, and they naturally create honor structures. But seeking praise

turns it into an idol. Be known by the quality of your work, and fix your desire for praise on God alone. Look forward to hearing from Him, "Well done, good and faithful servant."

2. **Stop being self-deprecating.** Again, this demonstrates weakness. Many men assume that it is somehow endearing to put themselves down; in fact, it shows that you lack confidence. Emphasizing and even apologizing in advance for your own failures or weaknesses rarely gains you anything. It merely draws attention to what might otherwise have gone unnoticed.

3. **Stop complaining.** Men solve problems. They don't whine about a situation; they create a solution with the resources available—including prayer. Complaining achieves nothing but to share your misery with everyone else. It demonstrates weakness of resolve, and typically reflects a victim mentality completely unbecoming of a man who was created to exercise dominion. It is also indicative of faithlessness: a man who complains implicitly sees himself over God, rather than under Him—demanding that his Father rule better, rather than trustingly submitting to His will.

4. **Stop making excuses.** If you fail, own it, and own it completely. Men are leaders, and leaders aren't excuse-makers. Owning your failure

demonstrates strength, because it shows that you will not sublimate your command over your world to anything—even when things don't go the way you wanted. Excusing failure is a demonstration of weakness, a willingness to become compliant to circumstance. It is seeking praise through the back door.

5. **Stop breaking promises.** Spurgeon observes, "Those who are quick to promise are generally slow to perform."[1] You break fewer promises if you are slower to make them. But if you say you'll do something, then do it. Do it no matter how hard it is. If you have a command of your world, then you know what you can and cannot do. So don't promise things you can't realistically do. Untrustworthiness might as well be a synonym for weakness. If you're not sure you can do it, or should do it, don't promise to do it. If you keep finding yourself breaking promises, then you don't have the command of your world that you thought, and you need to step back and re-calibrate. Always under-promise and over-deliver. (As a rule of thumb, assume that everything you're intending to promise will take three times longer and cost three times more than you expect.)

1. Charles Spurgeon, *John Ploughman's Pictures, or, More of His Talk for the Plain People* (Springfield, OH: Farm and Fireside, 1881), 10.

Subduing and ordering and cultivating yourself and your world *requires* strength, *requires* workmanship, and *requires* wisdom. It requires other things besides, but we assume you are acquainted with the Christian virtues in general—it is the uniquely masculine ones that concern us here. However, these virtues do not spring fully formed into you. We learn by doing. This means that although subduing and ordering and cultivating yourself and your world requires you to first *have* these virtues, doing so is also the only way to *produce* them. We have a chicken and an egg. How do we break into the cycle?

One way is by translating the virtues into manly obligations: a triad of duties that you can focus on, even if you have not yet developed the virtues they reflect very well. These duties naturally arise from the intersection of the three virtues, and like them, they are mutually defining and reinforcing. Because they are very broad, no single word captures their fullness, so we have arranged them as couplets:

1. The first duty is **envisioning and planning.** Put another way, this is having w*isdom about your workmanship.* Before a man can *do* anything he must know what his goal is. He must have a mission. This means not just undertaking to represent God in *principle,* but having a vision for how he personally will extend God's dominion and build God's house in

practice. He needs to know what the outcome will be and then start figuring out the specific steps he must take to achieve it.

2. The second duty is **building and supplying.** In terms of the virtues, it is w*orkmanship upheld by strength.* Whatever your plan is, however your mission looks, it will fundamentally be oriented at developing, equipping, and multiplying yourself, to extend God's rule into the earth. This includes physical production and *re*production: subduing and ordering your world to be suitable for a family; choosing and taking a wife to beget that family; then continuing to order your world so that those under you are never in need. But because the physical images the spiritual, you must also develop skill in spiritual building: ensuring that both you and those under you are progressing in establishing right order and right judgment by training them in righteousness.

3. The third duty is **guarding and fighting.** Think of this as *strength guided by wisdom.* This is a duty that bears extra emphasis in a world where we have forgotten that shepherds were like cowboys, capable of both shooting wolves and firmly handling sheep for their own good. Guarding is not merely passive, waiting to prevent something bad; it is active, ensuring the good. It means being watchful and alert—which circles back

around to planning: you must be proactive in guarding your vision, your direction, your path. You must be quick to fight for it. We have seen much lost, for instance, by men who relied too long on diplomacy and began fighting too late (discerning this, in turn, takes wisdom). What you are guarding and fighting for starts with yourself, and extends to those under you. Your job is to guide and protect yourself and your family for your mutual prosperity and unity. You take responsibility for them, and undertake to exercise authority over them: teaching, judging, correcting, and disciplining them and yourself.

At the intersection of the triad of duties there are particular *traits* that have been traditionally associated with masculinity. Although there are certainly many others we have not listed here, we consider these ones fundamental, because they are natural outworkings of the duties God made us for, and thus they also tend to represent paradigms of the virtues we should aspire to:

1. The first trait is **enterprise.** This combines the duties of *envisioning and planning + building and supplying* into a paragon of *workmanship.* Initiative, ingenuity, risk-taking—the vision and drive to establish something—these are classically masculine traits. As a man, you

should desire to be known for your enterprising nature. For example, too many men are content with being a passive employee to another man. Few hanker to develop their own productive property. This is not always because they lack enterprise; some men excel as lieutenants, as Joseph did under Pharaoh; but whatever your lot, you should be known for actively seeking to improve what God has placed you over. Enterprise is a grand word, but don't let that fool you—every grand enterprise has to start with a simple attitude of incremental improvement. Whether you're aiming for the stars or just adding a bit of value to your home, aspire to be enterprising.

2. The second trait is **constancy.** This combines *building and supplying + guarding and fighting* into a paragon of *strength.* Constancy means being able to stand firm and endure, under the strain of adversity, through changing circumstances, and over plain old time. It speaks to the traditional male traits of loyalty, faithfulness, determination, and stoicism. It is hard to underestimate the importance of constancy to a household. A constant man is not easily shaken or tossed about by changing winds; he takes his time and cannot be hurried when he knows that hurrying may cause him to trip. Bnonn spent many years training in historical European martial arts,

Michael in wrestling and boxing. Victory always comes down to controlling your man's position. This is done by taking his balance—and taking his balance is achieved by forcing his head off center. A man who flinches and bends his neck is a man about to receive a beating. If your family's head is not stable, its body is vulnerable. A woman who can rely on her man, who can rest assured in his consistency, diligence, and grit, is much more likely to be happy and content. Most women today are harried and anxious—because their men are flinching heads. You want flint, not flinch. Be a rock to those under your care.

3. The third trait is **readiness.** This combines *guarding and fighting + envisioning and planning* into a paragon of *wisdom.* Every man should be prepared for trouble or adversity, great or small. He thinks ahead. He is intentional about equipping himself to take charge of whatever scenario may arise, and he is decisive about dealing with it when it does. If things go south, he is ready to take care of the situation, and of those swept up in it—he does not expect others to take care of him. EDC (everyday carry) is an almost universally male hobby with good reason; readiness is a trait that is built into our DNA. But it is not limited to functional foresight, like always carrying a knife and a light; it is also

a spiritual discipline. A man should be ready to shepherd whenever the need arises; he should always be available to handle a problem that those beneath him cannot deal with. His station should make him *more* ready to serve by leading; not less.

These are traits, duties, and virtues that Scripture suggests as integral to manhood. By focusing on them, you can more easily order your life around God and learn to reflect His glory. The Bible speaks of worthless men; you must be the opposite. Perform your masculine duties and cultivate your masculine traits in order to develop the kind of virtue that makes you useful to God for the purpose for which He created you. Be of worth in exercising dominion. Be worthy of His name, to be called His son and image. In the process, you will get gravitas.

11 How to Bear the Weight

IT IS HARD TO EXERCISE DOMINION. THROUGHOUT history, even at the best of times and with the best of teachers, men have struggled. The curse on Adam affects all his children. Yet today, the burden men must carry can seem crushing. We have seen men buried beneath the weight of despair, frustration, and rage as they realize what they are up against.

In the movie *The Matrix*, the main character is presented with two pills: the red pill and the blue pill. If he takes the red pill, he'll awaken and see the world as it is. If he takes the blue pill, he'll stay "asleep" in the easy comforts of an artificial reality.

When he takes the red pill, he discovers that he is actually living in a brutal dystopian world.

This is a common analogy used for men in your situation. The red pill is the truth that society has been ravaged by feminism and fatherlessness, that you have been lied to about fundamental truths of sexuality, and that the Church has betrayed you for a kiss. Whether you are the son of an absent father or of a coddling mother, of a broken home or simply of our misandric culture, it is not a question of *whether* you have failed to launch but *how much*. Some opportunities are simply gone, and some goals are no longer achievable. Moreover, many *never* were achievable, despite what you were told. Much of God's good design is smothered and thwarted by forces you cannot overcome. When you realize everything you have lost, remember all the years you invested into efforts that were doomed to fail, and see the gross injustice of how the deck is stacked against you, it is a shock to the system. Typically, and rightly, you will feel an intense anger called "red pill rage."

A lot of men awaken to this reality only to stew on the raw deal they got. And, to be sure, modern men are victims of a twisted man-hating system. They are casualties of the war on gender: scarred, injured, and discouraged. We can relate. But you must realize that we aren't the first generation to be the product of failed fathers. Read through Judges 2 and you will find that there is nothing new under the sun. We can either learn from the failures of our fathers, and start correcting them, or we can extend those failures into the future and inflict the same or worse on our own sons. You can stay a victim, being all rage and no action—or you can take responsibility for yourself.

> Be angry and do not sin; do not let the sun go down on your anger, and give no opportunity to the devil. . . . Let no corrupting talk come out of your mouths, but only such as is good for building up, as fits the occasion, that it may give grace to those who hear. And do not grieve the Holy Spirit of God, by whom you were sealed for the day of redemption. Let all bitterness and wrath and anger and clamor and slander be put away from you, along with all malice. Be kind to one another, tenderhearted, forgiving one another, as God in Christ forgave you. (Eph. 4:26–32, ESV)

If you are on a trajectory to be a true patriarch, you will recognize the effeminacy of wallowing in red pill rage, egged on by the Absaloms of our day. On the contrary, a godly patriarch acts in faith—he behaves like Jesus really is exercising dominion, really is progressively ordering the world to make His enemies his footstool (Ps. 2; 110; 1 Cor. 15), and really does know what He is doing. You may well be angry, but remember that the anger of man does not produce the righteousness of God (Jas. 1:20).

We must only be angry as God is angry. Be angry, and do not sin.

This is truly difficult. Men who cannot get over their rage are stuck in a permanent "cage stage," feeding a vicious spiral of negativity in their echo chambers of choice. They are good for basically nothing; they have become worthless fellows. This is the origin of Men Going Their Own Way (MGTOW)—the very thing that Isaiah 53:6 says Jesus had to save us from. It is the origin of the self-loathing "black pill" community, where men race each other to the bottom in glorifying impotent passivity. In an upcoming chapter, we will talk about the power of brotherhood. Like all powerful things, brotherhood can be used for evil as well as for good. You need brothers around you who understand what you're going through. But there is great danger in seeking out "red-pilled" men, because they are often working through the same rage you are. Without grounded fathers to lead them, men in this kind of fraternity feed off each other in a way that can never produce the fruits of the spirit—peace, joy, contentment . . . and perhaps most importantly, hope.

Do not seek fraternity with men who are as angry as you are.

Seek fraternity with men who know your pain, but have made real progress in overcoming it, real progress in exercising dominion over their own lives. Seek men who are examples you wish to follow, men who will help you to fulfill Hebrews 12:12–15: "Therefore lift your drooping hands and strengthen your weak knees, and make straight paths for your feet, so that what is lame may not be put out of joint but rather be healed. Strive for peace with everyone, and for the holiness without which no one will see the Lord. See to it that no one fails to obtain the grace of God; that no 'root of bitterness' springs up and causes trouble, and by it many become defiled" (ESV).

Here's another way to look at it: if you want to learn to be a patriarch, to grow out of being a clueless bastard, you know by now that this starts by submitting yourself to the rule of your Father in heaven—not chafing against it. Whatever your personal mission is—and we will help you figure that out shortly—it will be subordinated to God's greater mission of calling all people to live the Christian life. In other words, you must faithfully receive how God has ordered both the world itself and your life so far. You must embrace His will that you start taking responsibility for what He has given you, even though it seems hard and unfair. Remember Job, and consider just how inadequate you are to answer back to God should He face you down out of the whirlwind.

The state of your life might not be entirely, or even mostly, your *fault*—but it is entirely your *responsibility*. That is what it *means* to be given dominion. Whatever you have dominion over—the state of that thing is on you. So you must choose to exercise dominion. You must decide that you will not be passive, that you will not be a victim. Our collective mission as Christians is to disciple the nations into obedience to all of God's laws (Matt. 28:19–20). How can we do that without first discipling ourselves in the same way?

God did not err when He wrote the book of your life. He made you for this time, He prepared the good works for you to walk in, and He fashioned your life to fit them (Eph. 2:10). Just as He made Nehemiah to rebuild Jerusalem with a sword in one hand and a trowel in the other, He made you to face down this wicked and perverse generation. Whatever your setbacks, there is still work that you can do—if you can keep faith, maintain hope, and let all that you do be done in love. It is up to you to accept your God-given duty. It is up to you to "man up."

Many callous feminists and manipulative pastors use "man up" as an incantation to get men to do what *they* want. We are using it as a call to do what *God* wants: the work of exercising dominion. You must man up, not out of some misplaced nobility about taking on a raw deal for the sake of women or society, but in order to image God Himself and play some part in *correcting* the raw deal.

Manning up is not easy. Even after you have dealt with the anger you feel, you will discover that exercising dominion doesn't come with palaces and throne rooms. It seldom even comes with heroics, and often not even with very much fun. It is mostly toil and grind. Thus, much of the difficulty you will face in living out what you know to be true revolves around how to be a doer of the word, and not a hearer only, deceiving yourself. All men enjoy talking about taking back dominion—but few get around to doing it. Most are like the sluggard of Proverbs 24: "I passed by the field of the sluggard and by the vineyard of the man lacking sense, and behold, it was completely overgrown with thistles; its surface was covered with nettles, and its stone wall was broken down. When I saw, I reflected upon it; I looked, and received instruction. 'A little sleep, a little slumber, a little folding of the hands to rest,' then your poverty will come as a robber and your want like an armed man" (vv. 30–34).

Fundamentally, a sluggard lacks sense (Prov. 24:30). He is a prolific consumer, craving and yet getting nothing (Prov. 13:4). He lives for weekends and snow days. "How long will you lie down, O sluggard? When will you arise from your sleep?" (6:9) Yet despite his uselessness, he is a know-it-all, "wiser in his own eyes than seven men who can give a discreet answer" (26:16). He is the kind of man who does little—but dreams much. Eventually his desire puts him to death, because his hands refuse to work (21:25).

We must not be like this. We have the word of God to instruct us. We have the Spirit of God to empower us. And we have the hope of eternal life to motivate us. We must not be sluggish in our faith. Yet even wannabe patriarchs often *are* sluggards. They want to man up—but they also *don't* want to.

This is a truly grueling difficulty, and we cannot downplay it. Understanding it is not only practically important but theologically and spiritually important as well. Why is it so hard for us to take responsibility? Why is it so hard to be doers of the word?

The answer, as usual, is in Genesis. Proverbs' observation of the nettles and thistles in the field of the sluggard points us there: "Cursed is the ground because of you; in toil you will eat of it all the days of your life. Both thorns and thistles it shall grow for you; and you will eat the plants of the field; by the sweat of your face you will eat bread, till you return to the ground, because from it you were taken; for you are dust, and to dust you shall return" (Gen. 3:17–19).

In *The Story of Sex in Scripture*, William Mouser explains, "In addition to the sentence of death, God curses the work of man and woman, that is, the productivity of their specific domains. Since Adam comes from the ground to work the ground, God curses the ground. It will be unproductive; labor will be hard. His own body will sweat as he struggles to make a living from a rebellious earth even as he journeys toward death, to return to the dust from which he was made."[1]

---

1. Mouser, *The Story of Sex in Scripture*, 20.

The curse creates quite the dilemma. By nature, each sex is driven to be fruitful in a way particular to their unique design. But the pursuit of that productivity always comes with the sting of the curse. Men want to cultivate a field—but that requires the hard work of overcoming thorns. Women want to cultivate a family—but that requires submission to a man and the pain of bearing children. Thus, the curse functions as an abiding chastisement to lead us to repentance. As we struggle to do what we are made to do, we are reminded that we live in a creation desperately in need of redemption.

In other words, we find in Genesis the reason that avoiding responsibility is such a temptation to us as men. The sluggard is a living embodiment of the curse. He didn't repair the wall when an animal kicked it over, or when the rain eroded it. He didn't remove the thistles and nettles when they were little weeds, and now they have overtaken the vineyard. He simply left it alone, and the earth reclaimed it. Think about that. The earth is ruling over the man, not the man over the earth. The dominion is backwards. It is an inversion of the creation design, on account of sin—the natural consequence of Adam inverting the creation order of dominion between himself, his wife, and God. As we noted in chapter 5, God's judgments are always perfectly fitted to the sin.

Now, of course, a vineyard can sometimes be in disrepair because of a terrible storm, a famine, a war, or some other disaster. There are many reasons for a man's life to be all jacked up, besides him being a sluggard. But we still know that, in most cases, the state of a man's lot is the result of his own decisions. Look back on the biggest mistakes of your life. How major a role did you play in those situations? Speaking for ourselves, a few weren't our fault . . . but the majority were. Either way, though, we were responsible for how we reacted to all of them.

To give an example, in 1989, a tornado wrecked Michael's grandmother's farm. It obliterated the chicken coop. It wrecked two of the barns. It destroyed ten acres of fencing. And it cracked the roof of their house. Things were in disrepair for a short season as they got their bearings. But within days, the rebuilding began—and within weeks, things were relatively back to normal. That tornado left wounds on their farm. But because of their diligence, those wounds were not fatal. So it is with any major personal crisis. It may make a mess—but we have a responsibility to diligently respond in faith. We mustn't be sluggards.

Yet it remains hard to take on this responsibility because being productive is cursed! The world pushes back as we push forward. We must toil at it. We know in our bones that there is a futility and pointlessness to it that can never be overcome. To take just the most trivial examples, you can't mow your yard just once. You can't discipline your kids just once. You can't weed your garden just once. It must be done over and over again. It must be maintained. It must be a habit. Because weeds and sins keep coming back.

The ease of the pre-fall world is no longer. We live in a fallen world that is cursed, and therefore full of difficulty. We naturally hate this.

In the past, most men had no choice but to exercise dominion. If they weren't productive, they died. But today, we are so wealthy, and our governments are so eager to pass around that wealth to those who will not earn it, that this problem barely exists. It is not only *easy* to be soft in the West, but our world is *designed* to actively make you soft, to make you a sluggard, to keep you living in the moment, putting off for tomorrow the hard things you could be doing today. You can literally live a life where every day you are fatter, poorer, and more dependent.

This naturally exacerbates our fatherlessness problem, and results in many men simply failing to start. It also makes correcting course much more difficult—there is not the pressing need of survival to force us to action. Being under the crushing weight of the curse, of God's law, has natural outworkings. The futility of labor turns dominion from something purely joyful into something that can be a real chore. We work all the days of our lives, and then at the end, for all our labors, we return to the dirt.

But a man does not escape the duty of dominion by refusing to perform it, any more than he escapes sin by refusing to obey the law. God *made* us to perform this duty. We *must* perform it; it is part of our very nature. A man who will not perform is not escaping the burden; he is merely laying another on top of it: the burden of kicking against the goads, of being constantly anxious and depressed because he knows he is a dead weight on society, a failure as a man, a powerless loser, and a sinner under judgment. No relief will be found by rebelling against our design. Work is, by nature, a source of happiness and fulfillment for men. Olympic runner Eric Liddell famously said, "I believe God made me for a purpose, but he also made me fast! And when I run I feel his pleasure." Conversely, one Korean study has found that while retirement does not increase rates of depression in women, it does in men.[2] Because we are workers.

This must be embraced. We must live the life God intended us to live. The curse makes it hard—but passivity and weakness destroy men in a way toil never can.

How do you treat work as a gift and a blessing and a joyful duty when it can feel like Sisyphus, pushing a heavy boulder up a mountain every day, only for it to roll back down? How can you be grateful about what seems like an unending, pointless grind? Like

2. Noh, Jin-Won, et al. "Gender differences in the impact of retirement on depressive symptoms among middle-aged and older adults: A propensity score matching approach." *PLoS One* 14.3 (2019): e0212607.

the Preacher, you might wonder, "For what does a man get in all his labor and in his striving with which he labors under the sun?" (Eccles. 2:22)

There is an answer. Part of that answer is finding a mission. But before you even do that, you must get out from under the *spiritual* weight. There is a way to lighten the burden of any work. Not that you can make it less difficult or toilsome. But you can redeem it. That is what the gospel does, because God rewards all work done in faith.

Jesus is the answer to the curse. This is not a health-and-wealth, seeker-sensitive motivational line. It is not meant to convince you that your life sucks less than it does (although, count your blessings all the same). It is a real solution to the burden of dominion. Because of Christ, we are no longer slaves, but sons. Paul writes: "When the fullness of the time came, God sent forth His Son, born of a woman, born under the Law, so that He might redeem those who were under the Law, that we might receive the adoption as sons. Because you are sons, God has sent forth the Spirit of His Son into our hearts, crying, 'Abba! Father!' Therefore you are no longer a slave, but a son; and if a son, then an heir through God" (Gal. 4:4–7).

If you are thinking this is "just" a spiritual change, that is the conditioning of neo-Gnostic evangelicalism talking. The Spirit changes *everything.* Theology has consequences. Because we are in Christ—who fulfilled the law, who performed what we never could, and who now exercises dominion from the right hand of the Father—we have everything He has. More than that, because we are in Christ, who died to the law—who is therefore no longer under it—we are freed from ever having to work to earn God's favor and gifts. God loves us in Christ and has already given us every possible treasure in Him. He is a Father. He has promised us an inheritance, and He is pleased to reward all His children.

And even more than that, some of the treasures He has provided for us are good *works.* The connection between works and workmanship is not a pun; it is theologically significant: "For we are His workmanship, created in Christ Jesus for good works, which God prepared beforehand so that we would walk in them" (Eph. 2:10).

God redeems our work, by working Himself through the Lord Jesus, to create new work for us. Thus, we should live not with a mindset of toil and futility, but with a mindset of abundance and reward. Again, Paul explains, "Slaves, in all things obey those who are your masters on earth, not with external service, as those who merely please men, but with sincerity of heart, fearing the Lord. Whatever you do, do your work heartily, as for the Lord rather than for men, knowing that from the Lord you will receive the reward of the inheritance. It is the Lord Christ whom you serve" (Col. 3:23–25).

All work done in faith for Christ has value, even the menial work of a slave—or, in the modern day, tediously filing TPS reports in a corporate cubicle. The value of this work is known by faith, not sight. It might not be realized in this life—but it is promised. God keeps His promises. And because we do this work, from the heart, for the glory of God, we are also freed from the burden of the approval of others.

A life set free by Jesus to live for the Father is a life set free from the weight of the curse. Regardless of your lot in life, you are able to say, "My yoke is easy and my burden is light." This is why, over and over again, we say, "Mission first, brothers." It is only by focusing on God's mission—the *missio Dei*—that we can truly order our lives and find fulfillment. And the *missio Dei* naturally brings your own mission with it.

12 Manhood through Mission

CHRIST EQUIPS YOU TO MAN UP WHEN YOU FOCUS on His mission. And the method He uses is to give you your own mission.

What does this mean? What do you actually need to *do?*

Let's start with what a mission is. It is really much simpler than many men imagine.

A mission is your best effort at wisely integrating your interests, skills, and circumstances into a personal vision for exercising dominion over what God has given you.

This dominion, of course, is exercised in God's stead. In a moment we will walk through some dos and don'ts for taking on this task, and you will see that it is actually very straightforward. Men were made to do it, so when it is explained to them, it naturally makes sense. But first we need to caution you against three assumptions that might tie you in knots.

The first is that your mission must be "spiritual." Modern Christians, conditioned into a functional gnosticism, think of serving the Lord as something that happens in church—so the ultimate version of this service is being a pastor, or maybe a mission-ary (*mission* is even in the name, after all). If they are not called to this, they think they are called to something lesser. As you now know, Scripture has a much broader and more holistic view of service than that. All of life is worship, and however you work, you are working for the Lord. Adam is the prototypical man, and being descended from him, we are to take over his work—his (co-)mission. So what does that look like?

Well, Adam's mission was not "spiritual" in the sense that modern Christians mean. He was to be fruitful (productive), to multiply and fill the earth (reproductive), and to exercise dominion (ordering the world). This certainly *was* spiritual, speaking in a biblical sense, where that term means something that involves man's spirit in cooperation with the Holy Spirit (cf. 1 Cor. 2:11–14). This is important to remember, because otherwise how could "mun-dane" work be worship? Naturalistic reductionism is no better than gnostic reductionism. But what we mean is that the primary work Adam was given, to till the ground, was notably ordinary and physical. Quite the opposite of what most people today mean when they speak of spiritual labor, Adam's mission was *vocational.* The work God gives him to do is just that: his daily *job.* So you, as a son of Adam, should be looking for a similarly vocational mission. The spiritual component of it will not be some kind of *separate* work, because ordinary labor *is* spiritual work when it is done in service of the Lord of Spirits, through the power of the Holy Spirit (Rom. 12:1–2).

The second assumption that will get you into trouble is the idea that your mission must somehow be epic. It is natural to *want* your mission to be the kind of thing that someone will later write a biography about, or make a movie to depict. This is, at root, a recognition that you are made for glory, that your place in God's plan *matters.* But this recognition is easily twisted by sin and, in the modern day, is blown out of all proportion, because your ideals have been conditioned by movies in which larger-than-life heroes achieve larger-than-life objectives—things that, in the real world, are just absurd. You are not Superman, or even Batman or John Wick or Dominic Turetto or John McClane. You won't be stopping any asteroids with your bare hands (or even with a nuclear bomb), or exposing any global conspiracies, or stopping any criminal masterminds. It is good to desire great things, but it is also imperative to be content with whatever lot God has given you. We must all seek to be like Paul, who learned to be content with much and content with little (Phil. 4:12). Aspire to be as great within your lot as you can be—but do not let foolish pride or unrealistic ambition blind you to the actual opportunities, and limitations, that God has placed before you.

Most importantly, the very first opportunity *and* limitation that sets the limits of your mission is your own conformity to God's law. Dominion over creation is pretty grand in principle, and it is true that Adam was made to rule as king in God's stead. But remember that Adam was made to be a *priest,* a servant, *before* he could become a king and a lord. It was only by obedient service that he could enter into the grandness of the plan that God had for him. This principle is consummated in the Lord Jesus, who, unlike Adam, did not count equality with God a thing to be grasped, but emptied Himself to become a servant, enduring the cross in order to attain the glory set before Him, despising the shame of it (Phil. 2; Heb. 12; cf. Matt. 4). This is why He tells us that the first shall be last, and the last first; He sets the example of it. The greatest things are generally given to those who first prove themselves worthy in the little. Even legendary journeys start with small steps—so do not despise the day of small things.

This point leads to another that we cannot possibly overstate: the danger of selfish ambition. While Adam's mission was glorious, he was incapable of achieving it by himself. He needed Eve, and more than that, he needed many, many children. It was only by *sharing* his glorious mission with his wife and progeny that he himself could *enter into* that glory. The grandness of his mission was inseparably communal. Therefore, you must be prepared to enter into mission with all those whom God gives you. The more jealously you guard your ambition, the more you treat your mission as "yours" rather than as a subsidiary of God's own mission, the less you will be able to perform it on your Father's behalf:

"Who among you is wise and understanding? Let him show by his good behavior his deeds in the gentleness of wisdom. But if you have bitter jealousy and selfish ambition in your heart, do not be arrogant and so lie against the truth. This wisdom is not that which comes down from above, but is earthly, natural, demonic. For where jealousy and selfish ambition exist, there is disorder and every evil thing. But the wisdom from above is first pure, then peaceable, gentle, reasonable, full of mercy and good fruits, unwavering, without hypocrisy. And the seed whose fruit is righteousness is sown in peace by those who make peace" (Jas. 3:13–18).

Not only is He *entitled* to give your mission to as many of His other sons as He pleases, but you should be *grateful* that He does. It conforms you closer to the image of Jesus, thus adding gravitas and glory to your own character, and it reflects back to God for His glory, which is the very purpose for which you are working in the first place:

> Make my joy complete by being of the same mind, maintaining the same love, united in spirit, intent on one purpose. Do nothing from selfishness or empty conceit, but with humility of mind regard one another as more important than yourselves . . . Have this attitude in yourselves which was also in Christ Jesus, who, although He existed in the form of God, did not regard equality with God a thing to be grasped, but . . . humbled Himself by becoming obedient to the point of death, even death on a cross. For this reason also, God highly exalted Him, and bestowed on Him the name which is above every name, so that at the name of Jesus every knee will bow, of those who are in heaven and on earth and under the earth, and that every tongue will confess that Jesus Christ is Lord, to the glory of God the Father. (Phil. 4:2–11)

Put simply, if you follow the flesh and work for your own glory, you will reap what you sow, and discover just how inglorious your flesh is. If you work for God's glory, truly staying on mission, you will discover just how glorious He is, and that glory will be added unto you—even if not in this world, then certainly in the next.

The third assumption likely to trip you up is that your mission must involve a detailed map of your life from here on out. Many men fail to start simply because they equate certainty about what to do with confidence of success. Then, since they lack that certainty, they assume they will fail—and so do not try to start.

We have observed that clueless bastards in particular are desperate for a paint-by-numbers clarity about every step they should take. This is why most modern books on masculinity are arranged in exhaustive categories and excruciating detail, as if life can be successfully engineered if only you get granular enough about breaking the process down. You may have noticed that we did not write this book in such a way. That was a careful decision, because your desire for a "system" is not a result of your father failing to teach you one. It is not a result of your father's refusal to show you how to map out your life. Maps like this don't exist. No man has one.

The reason you still want one is because you never learned how to use the compass of wisdom to navigate without one.

Think about this. God gave Adam a specific goal—but He did not give him a specific path to get there. He did not provide a Gantt chart or kanban board or timeline breakdown, pre-populated with every step of the program. Rather, He gave Adam

His Word, and His own image, so that he could learn to apply wisdom to his vocation, and achieve his mission through trial and error. This is important to reflect on, because while a mission should be specific, it does not require you to have mapped out each step for the next x years. A mission is not a *map*. It is more like a distant mountaintop, which you must figure out how to reach. This requires exploring the terrain to find a good route, and often it means using the compass of wisdom while the mountain is concealed from view.

With this in mind, we can start to talk about how to figure out what your mission should be.

The good news is that God has already given you everything you need to *start* working on this, regardless of your lot in life. He has given you specific interests, specific skills, and specific opportunities in the form of your life circumstances. This means that you only need to ask some basic questions to figure out a mission for your life. We recommend the exercise of asking these questions *even if* you already have a job, because a job and a mission, though tightly connected, are not identical. Your vocation will tend to reflect your mission, rather than vice versa. Many men start in one job but are led into another that suits them better. Others wisely try a number of options before making up their minds. It is not our intent to give you a complete handbook on choosing a vocation and connecting it to a mission, but we can give you some pointers to start moving in the right direction. We would highly recommend supplementing our advice by reading Rory Groves's *Durable Trades*.

Looking at your interests, skills, and opportunities is really all it takes to know God's will for your life. Although the *patterns* of providence will reveal His plans in more detail, this is a long-term and generally retrospective way of discovering them. And although dreams and visions are *possible*, they are exceedingly rare, and there is no reason to think you are so special that God will give you such a clear and straightforward view of what you should do. Rather, He "speaks" through the circumstances in which He has placed you, and through the principles of wisdom He has preserved for you in Scripture.

Your mission is your best effort at wisely integrating your interests, skills, and circumstances into a personal vision for exercising dominion over what God has given you. Start zeroing in on what this personal vision should look like by asking yourself a simple question:

What do you (or might you) like doing?

This is not, of course, a question about idle interests or casual hobbies. While you should feel free to put anything whatever on this list, even if you currently know nothing about it other than that it sounds interesting to you, pay special attention to skills you know you have. Don't worry yet about how you perceive their potential, whether they seem useful or lucrative, or anything like that. Rather, focus on where God has especially gifted you with strength, with wisdom, and with workmanship.

Given some time to reflect and brainstorm, you should be able to come up with a considerable list, and you will probably also find that there is significant overlap or commonality between many of the items on it.

At this point, you can start to filter, and there are three questions in particular you should be asking of each item you have identified:

1. Does it afford good opportunities to make money; can you see ways to use this to provide for yourself and for whatever family God gives you?
2. Does it afford good opportunities to love your neighbor? For instance, can you see ways to use this to advance the cause of your neighbor, consistent with God's law? Does it benefit others, or is it very inward-focused?
3. Does it afford good opportunities to glorify God? Can you do it really well, so that people who see it can see the excellence of God's handiwork? You may find that this question counterbalances question 2, and that is something to consider as you weigh your options.

Don't just look for obvious answers. God made us to be creative, like He is—to spot connections that other people don't see, and blaze new trails that no one has found before. If you have the chance to do this, why not take it? Ask yourself if there are areas where other men are not undertaking work that you think is important—work that fits with the questions above. Use the manly duties as a starting point, and think up questions of your own as you see fit:

- What needs to be planned or envisioned?
- What needs to be built or supplied?
- What needs to be guarded and fought for?
- What needs to be torn down or destroyed?

Although you will probably start your list with a large number of items, as you apply these kinds of questions, you will find that just a small selection rises to the top. These options will give you at least a pretty clear idea of the areas that God Himself would have you focus on in your life. You may find that an obvious answer pops out; if not, take the options to God, and pray for clarity and guidance as you seek to narrow down what you should do.

As you are doing this, consider what is perhaps the central pillar of a true mission, and the quality that distinguishes it from merely having a vocation: its *telos*. Start drawing a line between where you're at, and where you want to be at the end of your life. What is your personal mountaintop—the thing to which you are navigating? God has given you the compass of wisdom. It is up to you to map out where you're going as you explore. What comes in between the beginning and the end will fall into place as you take incremental steps toward your goal.

Ask yourself,

- What will your name stand for at the end of your life (Prov. 22:1)?
- What will it mean to come from or be a part of your household (Prov. 31)?
- How can you move towards this goal in some increment of time? Where do you want to be in one, three, five, seven years?

Write out three to five *end*-goals for the following areas:

1. Spiritual (devotions, knowledge of God, church, etc.)
2. Physical (health, sports, diet, etc.)
3. Economical (financial, assets, etc.)
4. Vocational (work, entrepreneurship, side hustles, etc.)
5. Relational (marriage, children, friends, etc.)

Your goals should be objectives that you believe are possible, but only with difficulty. Write them down, and then, once you have *some* idea of what God would have you do, write out an actual mission statement. Writing it out is a cliché for a reason:

putting your mission to paper really does matter. It makes your mission tangible and permanent, giving you something to hold yourself accountable to and measure yourself against. But write with a pencil. A mission is not carved into a monolith erected in your name for everyone to see. It is not immutable. It is a *best effort*—and unless you are completely stagnant, your best will be better next year than it is today. So you should feel completely free to update, adjust, or even entirely change your mission as you work to follow it, and as God reveals the path.

You should also feel free to write it however you like. One man may have a very clear mission tied to a single vocation; another may have an overarching purpose for his life that he works to fulfill through several different means. Working out how you want to connect the important elements in your own life is your decision; we are only pointing you to those elements, reminding you that they are important, and helping you to start being intentional with them so that you can get about the work of dominion for the glory of God.

The important thing is to have something to work toward—and then to simply *start*.

How?

Pick something. Pick *anything*. Just one thing that will move you just one step toward just one goal.

Then do it.

Repeat this process for the rest of your life.

It's that simple.

13 The Necessity of Fraternity

IT'S NOT ENOUGH TO BE *A* MAN ON A MISSION. The loner won't get far. "The rebuilding of culture," says Dr. Anthony Esolen, "is not going to happen without the reconstitution of brotherhoods."[1]

Think of your mission as a train. It requires rails to run on. The first of these rails is brotherhood. Without it, your mission will veer off course and eventually crash.

This reality runs directly against the individualism of our day that often masquerades as mature

---

1. Anthony Esolen, "Dr. Anthony Esolen: Who Burned Down the Culture, Why, and Now What?" interview by Patrick Coffin on *The Patrick Coffin Show*, podcast, episode 12, https://www.patrickcoffin.media/tonyesolen.

masculinity. We can see this especially easily if we consider how masculinity is portrayed in popular culture—and not just in goofy leftist mockeries of manhood, but in depictions that are taken as serious paradigms of the masculine psyche.

There is no better example than Clint Eastwood's final Western, *Unforgiven.*

The film opens on William Munny, a frustratedly incompetent hog farmer who, we learn, was once "a man of notoriously vicious and intemperate disposition." Shortly, he is visited by the Schofield Kid, an upstart hired gun, who wants a partner to help him collect the bounty on two cowboys that cut up a prostitute. But Will turns the offer down, saying, "I ain't like that anymore, Kid. It was whiskey done it as much as anythin' else. I ain't had a drop in over ten years. My wife, she cured me of that. Cured me of drink and wickedness."

This theme of being cured comes up repeatedly in the movie. While talking with his good friend, Ned Logan, Will regretfully remembers one of the men he murdered. Ned reminds Will that "you ain't like that no more."

Despite being "cured," Will is a shadow of his former self: old, tired, and unable to even rightly saddle a horse. No longer a deadly gunslinger, he barely subsists with his two children on his failing hog farm. And so the only way he sees forward for his household is to take one last job—even though he is unfit for the mission. He reluctantly agrees to help Schofield, on the condition that his old friend Ned can aid them in the undertaking.

Things do not go as planned. Schofield turns out to be unhelpful in a fight, as he is all but blind. Ned cannot bring himself to kill any longer. After muddling through the assassination of the two cowboys, Will turns ill. The town sheriff ruthlessly beats him, then tortures and kills Ned.

Will starts to drink again—and as he does, he slowly transforms back into the man he once was. He becomes a tough and focused loner, with a self-defined sense of justice. His new mission is revenge. Schofield recognizes that he is now truly dangerous, and fearfully offers the entire bounty to him. Will says, "You don't have to worry, kid. I'm not going to kill you. You're the only friend I got." Yet what he means by "friend" is not a brother-in-arms. Schofield is of no use to him. Will heads into town alone to get his revenge, and he single-handedly kills not only Little Bill but four of his henchmen too.

One of the noteworthy things about this movie is how Will evolves from what Ebert describes as a "contrite little boy" into an unstoppable man on a mission. This evolution happens as he becomes more and more isolated: wifeless, without a true friend, and far from his household.

It is not until the end of the movie that he truly becomes the "hero"—when he becomes deadly.

But is this a hero that men should aspire to emulate?

The idea of the isolation-powered antihero has become a trope in some of the most popular—and some of the darkest—modern entertainment. *John Wick* and *Breaking Bad,* for example, both follow in the footsteps of *Unforgiven,* teaching us that social ties pacify men. John Wick is more of an antihero, while Walter White is openly villain-ous—but both must be freed of the ties of frater-nity, marriage, and household in order to shine their brightest. Social isolation, we are told, is key to masculinity.

Our concern is less with these stories them-selves and more with the reasons for their pop-ularity. Why do they touch such a nerve in our culture? Many men lionize these characters. They do not perceive the lessons that the filmmakers themselves were perhaps hoping to convey. Instead they latch onto the idea that masculinity and isolation go hand in glove.

But the notion of becoming truly alone as the necessary catalyst to becoming truly self-sufficient, truly mission-focused, truly elite in commanding one's world, is a lie. It is a confusion.

Isolation *kills* mission.

Proverbs 18:1 says, "He who separates himself seeks his own desire; he quarrels against all sound wisdom." One commentary explains that this "de-notes a man who separates himself, for he follows his own counsel." This is a man who has untethered himself from community, so that he can pursue some selfish mission that will ultimately come to nothing. It is the fetishization of self-reliance.

God has made us to live in relationships. A man should be able to rely on himself—but "it is not good that the man should be alone." He needs both the right woman and the right men in his life. Together they are the two rails that keep his train on track. A tribe and a helpmeet will stabilize, direct, and magnify his mission.

It is deeply intuitive that a man should get a woman in order to achieve his mission. Men naturally want women, and indeed they judge each other by this. We will talk about this in the next chapter. But first, we need to cover something that has been essentially lost in the modern day—something that is no longer intuitive and is often seen as *un*natural:

Male intimacy.

There is a deep nonerotic intimacy that can and should exist among same-sex friendships. This intimacy is of a kind that cannot and will not exist among opposite-sex friendships. Take, for example, King David and Jonathan, the son of Saul. David eulogizes Jonathan, saying, "Your love to me was more wonderful than the love of women" (2 Sam. 1:26). Despite the twisted efforts of some modern interpreters, this isn't the king mourning his gay lover. No, it is David grieving the loss of a truly close friend and a fellow warrior. He repeatedly praises Jonathan for his exploits in battle, for the defense of Israel. Jonathan didn't back down from a fight.

He was swifter than an eagle and mightier than a lion (2 Sam. 1:22–23). He was that friend who stuck closer than a brother for David (Prov. 18:24).

Sexual *polarity* is what forms the strong bonds of marriage—but sexual *homogeneity* is what forms the strong bonds of friendship. There is a way of women, and a way of men; and while they have much in common, there are major differences. There are things about women that men will only understand in a theoretical sense, and the reverse is also true. Hence, women need a sisterhood; they need a close group united around shared emotion. But men need a brotherhood; they need a close group united around a shared mission. Men need other men with whom to participate in a common cause, fighting the same war. They need brothers who get it.

Despite movies like *Unforgiven*, the importance of brotherhood to masculinity can certainly be found in popular culture too. It is deeply ingrained in us, and stories that celebrate it ring true. Consider another famous Western: *The Magnificent Seven*. What made them magnificent, if not their fraternity? Individually, each was great in his own way but also a dysfunctional wreck in others. Not one of them alone could truly be called *magnificent*. Yet together, they polished over each other's flaws, filled in for each other's weaknesses, and combined each other's strengths.

In his article "Sometimes, I Miss War," Benjamin Sledge captures the male need for brothers on a mission: "I hated war, but strangely enough, I loved it, too. I'd find myself wishing I were back overseas while driving alone, or in the midst of a crowded party. Things were simpler. People understood me. I had deep relationships. Granted, there was no running water, and I defecated in a barrel on a regular basis. But the laughter was real, the friends were real, and the experience felt more real than ordering a coffee at Starbucks while a woman in athleisure berated the barista for getting her order wrong."[2]

Sledge didn't miss war because he was blood-thirsty. He missed it because he was brother-hungry. In war, he had a clear mission—and a fraternity that kept him company, kept him focused. He had a band of brothers, and in truth that mission and those brothers were more precious to him than his own wife. He writes, "Despite my resolve never to return to a combat environment, I'd signed up once more amid the height of insurgent violence. That deployment would cost me my marriage. I didn't even have to go. *I volunteered.* And all because my friends from Afghanistan were going. 'Would you jump off a bridge if all your friends were doing it?' my mother would chide as a teenager. 'Only if all my buddies from Iraq were jumping,' the now grizzled vet thinks."[3]

2. Benjamin Sledge, "Sometimes I Miss War," Human Parts, January 31, 2019, https://humanparts.medium.com /sometimes-i-miss-war-f2e248fd0e42.
3. Ibid.

Men need the love of men. We are all conditioned into a mindset today that would have been foreign and repugnant to men of old. We see David and Jonathan, and we suspect something is amiss. Their relationship looks "kinda gay." But it was not; they were dear friends. It is we who have something amiss. Men can be close—very close, like brothers, and even closer than brothers. Deep down, all men long for this brotherhood.

But brotherhood is not without danger. As we've already shown, sin can twist natural desires toward ungodly ends. So it is with brotherhood. Hence, Solomon warns his son:

> My son, if sinners entice you,
> Do not consent.
> If they say, "Come with us,
> Let us lie in wait for blood,
> Let us ambush the innocent without cause;
> Let us swallow them alive like Sheol,
> Even whole, as those who go down to the pit;
> We will find all kinds of precious wealth,
> We will fill our houses with spoil;
> Throw in your lot with us,
> We shall all have one purse,"
> My son, do not walk in the way with them.
> Keep your feet from their path,
> For their feet run to evil
> And they hasten to shed blood.
> Indeed, it is useless to spread the baited net

In the sight of any bird;
But they lie in wait for their own blood;
They ambush their own lives.
So are the ways of everyone who gains by violence;
It takes away the life of its possessors. (Prov.
1:10–19)

The wise king understands that his son's desire for mission, challenge, and brotherhood can be diverted down an evil pathway. It is natural for men to organize themselves into groups around shared missions. So the loner is an unnatural man who "quarrels against all sound wisdom." But not all bands of brothers are equal. Just as there is an evil patriarchy, so also there is an evil brotherhood, an evil fraternity. Such a gang is always tempting to men—but it is especially tempting when there is a dearth of good brotherhoods to join. The invitation to "throw in your lot" with men on mission, even if it is the wrong mission, is hard to turn down when you are alone. The longing for that shared mission, the desire to participate in the masculine drives of other men, is not to be underestimated.

Thus, every age has its gangs of violent men. They are inevitable in a sin-cursed world. Men are made for dominion, and dominion is a group project. Adam was told to be fruitful and to *multiply*. This was central to his work. In order to subdue the world, he had to first fill it. When Jesus expanded the creation mandate in the great commission, He addressed His disciples not as individuals, but as a congregation. Indeed, even the *focus* of this mission is communal; He did not say to make disciples *in* the nations, speaking of individuals, but to make disciples *of* the nations, speaking of vast brotherhoods, tribes, and tongues.

But as the wheat grows, so do the tares—and indeed, as we saw with Cain, weeds often grow faster than the crop. While the Lord Jesus raises up brothers who will band together in building His kingdom, Satan is busy stirring up his own sons who wish to do his desires instead. He was a liar and a murderer from the beginning, seeking to prey off the innocent and use creation to his own ends. So gangs of his sons destroy, rather than defend. They consume, rather than produce. Whatever God commands in the creation mandate, whatever can be discerned of His plan for men in their design, gangs twist and invert these. They rape instead of marrying. They occupy instead of building. They threaten instead of protecting.

Do not fall in with this kind of group. It should go without saying that they will not improve you; they are a crooked rail that leads to destruction. Do not be deceived; a gang can destroy, consume, steal, rape, occupy, and threaten—without *seeming* like a gang at all. Remember that not all acts of murder, theft, and adultery are overt. They start in the heart and are easily justified (Matt. 5). Know what they look like as seeds, before they grow into thorns that will choke you.

We warn you gravely about this only because the need for brotherhood is itself very grave. We must recover fraternity if we are to recover sexual sanity. It is not just that you need it emotionally. It is not just that you need it to exercise dominion over the world. You also need it for the most basic piety. You need it to exercise dominion over yourself. Correctability is the single best weapon a man can wield in his battle against effeminacy and for manliness—and correctability primarily happens through the bonds of brotherhood.

The iron cannot be made harder apart from the fire and the blacksmith's blows. So it is with men. The man that spurns correction will remain soft and fragile. This is why Proverbs repeatedly commends correction as something that produces vitality: "Correction and instruction are the way to life" (6:23, NIV) and "whoever heeds life-giving correction will be at home among the wise" (15:31, NIV).

No correctability means no virility.

How do you become correctable? Brotherhood provides the context in which it can happen naturally, without animosity. We have all had bad breath before but not realized it. In the same way, we can only see many of our sins and problems through the eyes of others—but they must be others we have strong bonds with, men we trust who are not faux friends, nor frenemies, but brothers who will receive our correction in turn. This is why Proverbs 27:17 says, "As iron sharpens iron, so one man sharpens another."

This sharpening is a natural part of masculinity. It is built into us in a unique way. You may have noticed that men insult each other and don't mean it. In fact, insults are a natural way that men bond and show affection. Women are quite different. They *compliment* each other and don't mean it. When they insult each other, it's serious. Men can fight and be friends afterwards; women become bitter enemies. As a general rule, men bond by a process of exclusion; women by a process of inclusion.

This is to be expected since we are designed for different things.

For men, because we are designed to work together to subdue the outward world, to get on mission together, testing each other is critical. It is how we can establish a working hierarchy. Every man must test and ensure his place by competing within the group.

Women are designed for different work: to fill the inward world, building a community. Thus, connecting with each other to establish social harmony is critical. Every woman must ensure her place by fitting into and conforming within the group.

Because of this, meritocracies like true aristocracies, classical democracies, or biblical monarchies are masculine ideals. Feminine forms of government include flat democracies (everyone is equally

competent), oligarchies (cliques), and commit-
tees (no one is responsible). This is how we get the
Church Effeminate, as we discussed in chapter 5.

Male friendships also tend to be more robust
than female ones. They don't fall apart as easily
when subject to stress, because they are to some
extent built on stress to begin with. They are designed to thrive under the difficult conditions of
mission. A famous depiction of the power of male
friendship is Apollo and Rocky pushing each other
to the absolute edge of their abilities. Another (less
famous) example is Bnonn and Michael's friendship. This book, and our ministry, would not—
could not—exist without the partnership between
us. Neither of us could have built it without the
complementary skills and knowledge of the other—and neither of us could have weathered the
opposition we have received without the counsel
and support of the other.

"Two are better than one because they have
a good return for their labor. For if either of them
falls, the one will lift up his companion. But woe to
the one who falls when there is not another to lift
him up. Furthermore, if two lie down together they
keep warm, but how can one be warm alone? And
if one can overpower him who is alone, two can resist him. A cord of three strands is not quickly torn
apart" (Eccl. 4:9–12). This has application to both
fraternity and to marriage—but the explicit context
is fraternity. Good male friends will support you,

complement you, shield you, raise you up, push you forward, pull you back when necessary, hone you, critique you, and ultimately sanctify you. Men need men. Find each other. Take risks. It's worth the reward.

That said, not all the criticism and correction you will receive is likely to be well-intentioned. Some will not be even remotely true. As you start to develop self-discipline, as you start to pursue mission and order your life well, your efforts will be ill-received by some—often the very men you *hope* to forge fraternity with. Like crabs in a barrel, as one tries to escape, the others try to drag him back down. So while some men will be impressed and inspired as you start to become a better man, others will become envious and self-loathing—the crabs. You will become a lightning rod for their effeminacy and negativity as they look for ways to take you down a peg.

Crab mentality is just envy. As the 1828 Webster's puts it, they "feel uneasiness, mortification or discontent, at the sight of superior excellence, reputation or happiness enjoyed by another." Envy is the key motive behind "haters." And there is no avoiding haters, because envy lives in the heart of every man.

It is easy, reading this, to muster the bravado to dismiss haters. The problem is, in real life, you will be affected by it—because of the power of brotherhood. Many men who want to get on mission spend their lives with one foot hovering over the gas, the other tapping the brake, because they're afraid that they might actually be successful—and then everyone will discover that they are frauds and pounce on them. You need to get over this. You may not live up to the hype, but that's no reason not to step up to the plate. There are specific things you can do to prevent anyone pulling you back into the barrel:

1. **Repent of your own envy.** At some level, we all are envious haters. Envy leads to disorder (Jas. 3:16). So escaping the crab barrel, re-ordering your life, begins with repenting of your own envy and covetousness. Your first spiritual habit should include recognizing and mortifying envy when it arises in your own heart.

2. **Don't tell people you're making changes until you have established a true habit.** Don't talk about it. Just do it. Proverbs 14:23: "All hard work brings a profit, but mere talk leads only to poverty" (NIV). *Acta non verba.* A mere talker invites mockery—but it's hard to mock a doer. It's easy to go to the gym for a week, or practice family worship for a month. Big whoop. It's also easy for others to hate a braggart and a dilettante—so don't be one. Focus on the work.

3. **Start smaller than you want to.** Sudden drastic changes not only tend toward failure, but

they also draw unnecessary attention to your efforts. It will trigger crab people. We have found that small changes are best, because they go unnoticed until significant things have been accomplished.

4. **Receive correction even if you suspect it is motivated by envy.** Remember that you lose nothing by hearing a false correction and gain much by hearing a true one—even if it is given out of wicked motives. It is always possible that you are in the wrong. Other men don't trust a defensive man; it shows that he is brittle. They do trust a reflective man. If your critic was wrong, he'll come to see it in time. There is certainly a time to defend yourself; the apostle Paul defended his ministry vigorously on occasion. But you must be willing to spend time as the anvil, not just as the hammer.

5. **Do all your work unto the Lord.** This is the foundation on which all the other points rest. Those that live for the praise and notice of men will never escape the crab barrel. The little verbal jabs of crab people will injure their pride and cause them to tumble down. Not so with those that labor for God. Your efforts to change will be derailed if you get caught up with proving yourself to crab people. Don't try to please them. Pursue change in a spirit of humility for the glory of the Lord. "Humble

yourselves in the presence of the Lord, and He will exalt you" (James 4:10).

In his book *The Way of Men*, Jack Donovan rightly says, "There is a difference between being a good man and being good at being a man."[4] In other words, you can possess the skills of manhood but lack the virtues of a godly masculinity. Such a man was Cain. He was a city-builder—but also a brother-killer. He built for his own name, not for the name of God. He was masculine—but evil.

The converse cannot be true, however. You cannot be a godly man, without also being good at being a man. Again, Donovan keenly observes, "To protect and serve their own interests, the wealthy and privileged have used feminists and pacifists to promote a masculinity that has nothing to do with being good at being a man, and everything to do with being what they consider a 'good man.' Their version of a good man is isolated from his peers, emotional, effectively impotent, easy to manage, and tactically inept."[5]

For the evil patriarchy to succeed, they must keep men pacified and isolated from each other. A mass of unified, principled, and disciplined men is a threat to evil kings—and to the kingdom of darkness.

4. Jack Donovan, *The Way of Men* (Milwaukie, OR: Dissonant Hum, 2012), 79.
5. Ibid, 82.

You need a gang of men. You need men who will correct, improve, and push you. Not insecure crabs, but a brotherhood committed to godly excellence. Take to heart the wisdom of Paul when he exhorts Timothy to "flee youthful passions and pursue righteousness, faith, love, and peace, **along with those** who call on the Lord from a pure heart" (2 Tim. 2:22, ESV, emphasis added).

Flee sinful effeminacy, pursue godly masculinity, and do it with brothers in the Lord.

14 The Excellence of Marriage

"HE WHO FINDS A WIFE FINDS A GOOD THING and obtains favor from the Lord" (Prov. 18:22). Nothing can multiply a man's mission like a good wife. And nothing can consume it like a bad one.

Only a man and woman together can fulfill the creation mandate. You cannot build a household without a good woman at your side.

It is a key milestone for a man, and a massive step forward, when he finds a wife. She is the second rail, running parallel to fraternity, that supports him, carries him forward, and keeps his mission on track.

If she is straight and true.

Much is made, and rightly so, of the virtuous woman in Proverbs 31. But often overlooked is the fact that Proverbs 31, following the book as a whole, features *two* kinds of women: one virtuous and rare, the other wicked and common. The former is Lady Wisdom: a productive magnifier of her husband's strength, who pursues their mutual glory by building his house. The latter is Lady Folly: a wanton woman who consumes her husband's strength in pursuit of her own wayward lusts, and so "tears it down with her own hands" (Prov. 14:1). Chapter 31, as the climax of Proverbs, rightly focuses on Lady Wisdom as the prize to be gained by rightly navigating the treacherous waters of your fallen masculine drives. She is a prize simultaneously symbolic, representing wisdom and good character, and archetypal, representing the ideal wife.

But verses 1–3 contain one last warning to not trip over Lady Folly as you're approaching the finish line:

> The words of King Lemuel, the oracle which his
>   mother taught him:
> What, O my son?
> And what, O son of my womb?
> And what, O son of my vows?
> Do not give your strength to women,
> Or your ways to that which destroys kings.

This is not a warning against giving your strength to *a* woman. Men are designed to give their strength to *a* woman because a good wife is a strength-magnifier. The man is the house-builder; the woman the home-maker. She takes that house and she appoints it and furnishes it until it becomes a home: a place of rest and comfort and hospitality. The man is the supplier; the woman the refiner. She takes the raw materials that he provides through the sweat of his brow—whether food, or cloth, or money, or whatever else—and returns them as a good meal, a fine garment, a beautified home, or some other resource of greater value. This is most exemplified in child-bearing itself, where she takes her man's seed into her, and returns it to him as an offspring and an inheritance.

Thus, Lemuel's mother cannot be warning him about giving his strength to *a* woman—but rather, she is cautioning him against letting the powerful instinct to do so drive him to give his strength to *any* woman.

There are many women who will take a man's strength and consume it. These are the kinds of women of whom Proverbs 7:26–27 says, "For many are the victims she has cast down and numerous are all her slain. Her house is the way to Sheol, descending to the chambers of death." Many men can testify to the hell it is to be married to an ungodly woman. The best path is always to avoid her altogether. Hence, Proverbs says, "Do not stray into her paths" (7:25)—lest she become like a constant dripping on a day of steady rain (27:15). "An excellent wife is the crown of her husband, but she who shames him is like rottenness in his bones" (Prov. 12:4).

All this is just another application of the principle we have seen before, that the greater and more glorious something is made to be, the more destructive and awful it becomes when perverted by sin. Many so-called patriarchalists, overreacting to real perversions, seem to doubt that good women actually exist—let alone great ones. At best, they will grant feminine virtue on paper; but what they allow in principle they deny in practice, generalizing all women into a negative average. The common AWALT trope—"all women are like that"—infantilizes and vilifies them as a sex, and refuses to endorse marriage because of some assumed probability of a negative outcome. But Scripture affirms that the only reason it is *possible* for women to be so appalling, so worthy of contempt, the cause of such bitterness, and the bringers of such ill repute upon their sex . . . is because God made them to be the glory of man—the very pinnacle of creation—and that such glorious women *really do exist*.

An excellent wife is a truly great blessing, a truly glorious crown in whom a husband can rejoice and boast before kings—not just in the pages of Scripture but in the book of creation too.

This is why, for most young men, libido is over all. Sex is the most powerful and constant drive in our lives precisely *because* it is engineered to propel us toward the most valuable and worthwhile blessing for our mission: a woman, a helpmeet, a marriage.

But it is exactly on this point that men make a terrible mistake—so we need to circle back to the analogy of the railway track.

We said before that there are two rails on which your mission runs: fraternity and marriage. There is an important and much-overlooked implication of this, which requires your careful attention:

Since a wife is a *complement* to your mission, she *cannot be the mission itself.*

Just as a band of brothers is not your mission, but a support to it, so a wife is not your mission, but a support to it.

This is really, really important.

To understand why, let's go back one last time to Genesis. When God made Adam, He gave him a mission. To complete this mission, Adam needed a helper. The order of events is significant: God commissioned Adam *first;* then God created Eve and brought her to him. This creation pattern reveals two key principles about God's general design:

1. Men should generally have a mission before they seek a wife to magnify it.
2. Women will generally desire a man who is already on mission—a man who can carry her along because he is already going somewhere.

This is why we have structured this book as we have. Getting a wife is a good thing. Scratch that—a great thing. It is *good* to be a husband. But it is good to be a man *first.*

Unfortunately, many men today become husbands and fathers *before* they figure out manhood; because they are clueless bastards, they are not guided and supported into maturity by other men who can encourage them into a mission and keep them on track while they establish themselves. They do not go through this process at all, and so they instead default to instinct—and the strongest instinct is to get a woman. Indeed, because of the curse and the burden of performance, the strongest instinct is to get a woman while *avoiding* mission.

Without fathers and brothers to push him on mission, a young man's instincts—if he wants to avoid fornication—push him into marriage instead. But the need for mission does not disappear, nor the need to validate his manhood. So without fathers and brothers to guide him into a larger goal, and validate him as a man, he tends to fill these voids with his wife. "See, I'm a man because I got a woman. I achieved my mission and got a wife. She wants to have sex with me. This all proves that I'm a man."

This creates many an unhappy marriage. The more a man relies on his wife to validate his masculinity, and the more his direction in life centers around her, the more needy of her he becomes— but the more needy a man is of a woman, the less attractive he is to her. Neediness signals the opposite of dominion, the opposite of responsibility and authority and ability. The man begins to treat his wife not as a helper but as a mother. This creates a vicious spiral of increasing disaffection: less sex, less togetherness, less sense of mission, less confidence in each other, and for the man, less mastery over his world and less belief in his manhood. Hence the Hollywood trope of the buffoon dad, who is functionally just another one of the children.

Some men are able to escape from this cycle once they realize what marriage has gotten them into. They got the woman, they got the sex—but now they have to provide. They therefore find themselves forced to mature as men—to get on a mission, to exercise dominion. Usually they will resist this, doing the bare minimum, until children come along. Fatherhood is often the catalyst they need to really start scrambling into their masculinity. But even when this happens (and it does not always happen), it is 180 degrees off the way it should be, and is often too little, too late. They do start growing into the right mindset—the mindset that should have *produced* fatherhood—but they often simply don't have the time or guidance to turn the ship around before their marriages implode.

Proverbs 24:27 says, "Prepare your work outside and make it ready for yourself in the field; afterwards, then, build your house."

You need to do some work on your "field" and prepare the raw materials, before you take a wife to build your house.

Stated concisely, **chase excellence, not women.**

It is not surprising so few men figure this out. Compounding the dearth of fraternity, the media for generations have been pushing precisely the reverse message. The correct order is to get on mission, *then* find a woman to complement you, but popular culture teaches men exactly the opposite. In addition to the bozo father role models you'll see in many movies and popular TV shows, music has been a key vector for indoctrinating men into this "beta" mindset. Take, for instance, the words of a 1930s crooner in "I Don't Want to Set the World on Fire":

> In my heart I have but one desire
> And that one is you
> No other will do.
> I've lost all ambition for worldly acclaim
> I just want to be the one you love
> And with your admission that you feel the same
> I'll have reached the goal I'm dreaming of.[1]

Along the same lines, we have again been taught by popular music, Disney movies, and even women's porn (romance novels), that there exists only a single woman in the world who is "the one," the perfect soulmate for us—who, should we lose her, could never be replaced, and would forever leave

---

1. "I Don't Want to Set the World on Fire," music and lyrics by Sol Marcus, Edward Seiler, Bennie Benjamin, and Eddie Durham, 1938, lyrics © Ocheri Publishing Corp., Bennie Benjamin Music, Inc., Ocheri Music Publishing Corp.

a gaping void in our lives. Placing a woman on a pedestal like this, thinking of her as "the one" is enormously destructive and actually reflects the vestiges (and possibly return) of pagan thinking in our culture. It is yet another variant of androgyny and actually comes from ancient monistic myths where humankind was originally made as weird four-armed, four-legged beings that were split in two by the gods—each half being cursed to search out the other in order to be complete again. This kind of paganism appears in more sophisticated forms in the modern day. For instance, many esoteric teachings will reinterpret the fall as the failure of ideal androgynous beings to balance the masculine and feminine polarities in themselves, with a subsequent loss of enlightenment beginning the process of reincarnation in male and female forms. But whatever trappings are added to it, the underlying idea is the same: male and female are incomplete in themselves, and typically, there is only one "other half" out there that perfectly matches you.

All pure, utter garbage. Satan's strategy is always the same: cut the Creator down to size by eliminating the distinction between Him and His creation. And this always has the same follow-on effects: of eliminating *all* created distinctions, claiming that they are not good parts of God's design, but results of the fall. Ultimate reality, perfected reality, Satan would like us to think, eliminates all distinctions into an undifferentiated oneness.

This idea has wormed its way deep into the modern Church. It is not so much explicitly stated as implicitly taken for granted that "true love" eliminates all loneliness, and that to find one's soulmate is to become complete. Connected with this, true love takes on divine power, replacing the marriage covenant as the sanctifier of sex. But God designed sex to image *covenant* love—not *romantic* love. The covenant love within marriage certainly does involve romance, but it is the *covenant* that sanctifies the sex, *not* the romance. Romance doesn't purify sex, and sex without romance is not dirty. *Marriage* purifies sex, and sex without *marriage* is dirty. Unfortunately, this is no longer widely accepted in the Church. And once romance becomes all that is required to legitimize sex, fornication becomes inevitable.

Theology has practical consequences. And practice has theological consequences. The Western Church has tacitly reversed the relationship between marriage and what it symbolizes. Gyneolatry, the functional worship of women, has been the inevitable result. Marriage is God's picture of the perfect onetogetherness we will ultimately experience in communion with Him. *That* is the reality it points to. To flip this around and make marriage the fulfillment of this reality is, in fact, straightforward blasphemy.

We emphasize this so you'll understand why you must chase excellence rather than women. You especially cannot become stuck on a single woman as the one you absolutely must marry and without whom you simply cannot be happy. Whether you get her or not, such a mindset will lead you into shipwreck. Anyone who thinks of their spouse as the "other half" that *completes* them is setting up their marriage for failure. No spouse can ever fulfill all of your needs because no spouse was made to. Imagining otherwise leads to ever-increasing discontentment and heartache, instead of what you should see in a healthy marriage, which is the opposite of discontentment and heartache. Not only this, but such a mindset will rationalize divorce where Scripture forbids it, since the spouse "wasn't my soulmate"—as proved by the fact that the marriage turned sour! *No* woman will ever "complete" you; neither will you complete her. No woman can ever fully satisfy you; neither you her. Only God can. It is normal and generally healthy to become attached to—dare we even say a little smitten by—an attractive woman whom God places in your path, once you determine she would make a good wife. But it is also immensely easy in the modern day to become irrationally besotted, and we must warn you that this is not only unmanly but also ultimately ungodly. It reflects a deep-seated theological idolatry that, if you drag it out into the light of day, you will find abhorrent and immediately wish to put to death.

Such idolatry ends up placing your locus of control on your wife—and thus also your locus of dominion and virtue. It is impossible for a man to gain gravitas this way. He will not so much become virtuous and gain gravitas as he will become like William Munny from *Unforgiven*—domesticated by his wife's expectations. As Ebert put it in his review, "violent men are 'civilized' by schoolmarms, preachers and judges"—the very problem we are now facing on a global scale. You do not want to be civilized in this way, becoming, as Ebert said, a "contrite little boy." On the contrary, you must exercise dominion over your drives to become a man of *holy* violence, the kind of man who seizes the kingdom of God by force (Matt. 11:12)—for the good of himself, of his wife, and of his entire house.

It is true that it is not good for a man to be alone. God makes a point of illustrating this; Adam needs a helper "opposite to him" (Gen. 2:20, literally). The Hebrew words carry the connotations not only of facing him as a reflection but also of inversely corresponding to him; "helper" is *ezer*, meaning one who does for another what he cannot. But *inability* is not *incompleteness*. Separately, Adam and Eve are both complete in themselves; they are fully formed people who lack nothing in their intended manner of imaging God. It is rather that this intended manner is distinct to their sexes, and thus it is incomplete with respect to the purpose of humanity taken as a whole—of completely ordering the world as God desires. Roughly speaking, Adam can subdue but not fill; Eve can fill, but struggles to subdue. Together, they supply what the other lacks and perfect the other's natural virtues, duties, and abilities, to bring right order to every sphere of life. The picture is of two facing parts that, while functional and complete in themselves, also fit together in such a way that they become a greater whole. Alone, neither one of them can carry God's dominion into the world. Together, they can—by filling out what the other lacks. So it is not a question of finding a missing half—it is a question of finding a complementary help. There is nothing missing or incomplete in the man as a person; rather, there is something missing and incomplete in what he can achieve alone. The same is true of the woman.

To bring it back to your particular circumstance, you do not need a wife to complete *you;* you need a wife to complete your *mission.*

But let us now point out something that should be obvious yet often isn't:

If you don't know what your mission is, you cannot really assess whether a particular woman will make a good helper for it.

Finding and pursuing a godly mission should come before finding and pursuing a godly wife; the latter is not even a *sequential* goal, but a subordinate one. Pursuing a godly wife is simply one step—an especially important step, to be sure—in pursuing your mission.

Because this is the design, it should come as no surprise that being on mission also makes finding and pursuing a godly woman a lot easier. You will be far more likely to be successful, and far more likely to attract a higher-quality woman—because women are attracted to men on mission. When you make achieving the *mission* your mission, you are comparatively more likely to find a wife and achieve the mission. When you make achieving *marriage* your mission, you are less likely to find a wife, and you will achieve very little else besides.

Think of it this way: a woman is looking for a good leader. But a leader isn't just someone people follow. He is someone they believe will take them where they want to go. To lead, you must have a vision of where you are going, a mission that you're working toward. If your mission is no more than getting a wife, where are you leading *her*? To herself? No sane, holy woman will want to marry a man who is functionally leading her to herself. No sane, holy woman wants a man tacitly deifying her.

This is why we have spent the majority of this book introducing you to being a man, to being on mission, and are only now talking about marriage. Getting a wife really does logically come *after*. You don't want to be playing catch-up once you're already married, feeling like a phony—and neither do you want to find yourself unable to attract the quality of woman that every good Christian man wants. No matter how good your "game," you will have far better odds of attracting a good wife if you have first taken time to develop yourself into the kind of man that every good

Christian woman wants. You want enough gravitas to draw that kind of woman into your orbit. *Any* man can get *a* woman—just check out your nearest red-light district. But if you want a Proverbs 31 woman, rather than Lady Folly, you are going to have to work a lot harder on yourself. Such women will naturally gravitate to men who can demonstrate godly dominion. So you must develop gravitas.

But it is not just *women* who gravitate to such men. Other men do also. This is why we placed fraternity before marriage: gravitas is primarily signified through your relationships with other men. Mission is achieved with other men. Women are attracted to men whom they see other men wanting to honor and follow. Status and mastery in a masculine hierarchy are clear signals that you are to be desired for a husband.

The upshot for you is that it's much easier to "find" a godly wife when you have "prepared your field." A man on mission is simply more attractive. Consider: If a man tells another man that he is dating a new girl, one of the first questions will be, "What does she look like?" If a woman tells another woman that she is dating a new guy, one of the first questions will be "What does he *do*?"

Looks matter for ladies—but the mission matters more. Nice guys finish last, and jerks get the girl, not because girls like jerks, but because they like men on mission. The nice guy thinks he should make the woman his mission. He puts her on a pedestal—which means he demotes his mission in favor of her. The jerk doesn't. His independent drive supersedes her—and that attracts her.

Subconsciously, no woman wants the burden and stress of being a man's center. At a deep level, she knows it would make them both miserable. Moreover, because she knows herself, she cannot help despising a man who would settle for such a mediocre vision. She wants to help him work toward something greater than both of them, as she was designed to do—not watch passively as he works for something no bigger than herself.

The takeaway isn't to be a jerk. Men should be kind and humble—but absolutely driven. Nothing can get in the way of the mission. This not only attracts potential spouses but also works as a filtering system: "Marrying me means joining my mission. If you won't join, then this won't work."

Before Michael started officially dating Emily, he told her: "I like you. I want to get to know you. But you need to know I feel a call to the ministry. I'll be hated, probably poor, and away from home a lot. If that's a problem, this won't work." That was twenty years ago. He stayed on mission. He got the girl.

Don't think we are saying that figuring out your mission is a silver bullet for finding a wife. We know how hard it is out there compared to just a generation ago. But mission is where you should *start*, and focusing on it will increase your odds. God has given you gifts. How can you use them to give

Him glory and expand His kingdom? What vocation is a good use of them? What skills and disciplines do you need to develop to excel in that vocation? Pursue them with singleness of mind. Be patient; do not be deceived by the illusion of the short term. God is faithful. What a man sows, so shall he reap in due time.

Do not give your strength to women nor to anything else that will consume it instead of magnifying it.

Do not be harnessed, pacified, or destroyed; rather, build yourself up, and start working to exercise dominion over yourself and your world.

Everything else will follow from that.

Afterword

EVERY BOOK HAS TO START SOMEWHERE. Every book has to include what it can. And then every book has to end somewhere too.

In writing this book, we were not trying to create a timeless work but a timely one. A thousand things went through our minds as we were planning it. A thousand more as we were writing it.

We know that many a husband and many a father is burning with unanswered questions about being better in these duties. Similarly, many a single man is burning with questions about more practical ways to attract a wife.

We wanted to cover all these things; but if we had written on everything that was worthy of inclusion, we would never have finished this book, let alone published it—and no one would have read it anyway.

We had to be firm in our goal and disciplined in cutting anything that didn't achieve it—no matter how important to the topic of manhood more generally.

Our goal has been to give every man a place to *start*.

Whether you are single, married, or divorced, young or old, wealthy or broke, driven or listless, starting out or starting again, you have to start somewhere—and that is with being a *man*.

So being a man is what this book is about. Not about being a husband. Not about being a father. Being a man.

Marriage, sex, and fatherhood follow from this, and we intend to write on them also. But the need of the day is for men to be men—to have at least a basic foundation on which to build Christian marriages and to raise up godly seed.

We hope this book has given you that foundation. It is only a place to start—but starting is everything. There is much more that we want you to know, but what you now know should be *enough*.

Get out there and use it. The kingdom of God consists not in words, but in power. Yes, misandry is real. Yes, society is messed up. But now that you understand the problem, and God's design for you as a man, will you stay a victim—or will you fight alongside our great and awesome God? We exhort you not to despise the day of small things. Start little, build big. This is how God works, especially in periods of restoration. We are living in such a time.

Patriarchy is inevitable. It is not whether men will exercise dominion, but which ones, and how. Choose this day to be such a man and to rule in the stead of your Father God.

Take courage, brother. Be what God made you to be: a man.

It is *good* to be a man.

MICHAEL FOSTER &
BNONN TENNANT